TOP10
LOS ANGELES

Top 10 Los Angeles Highlights

Welcome to Los Angeles..............**5**

Exploring Los Angeles...................**6**

Los Angeles Highlights...............**10**

Historic Hollywood Boulevard.....**12**

Sunset Strip..................................**14**

The Getty Center.........................**16**

Los Angeles County
Museum of Art (LACMA)..........**20**

El Pueblo de
Los Angeles.............................**24**

The Huntington **28**

Universal Studios
Hollywood^{SM} **32**

Griffith Park.................................**34**

Disneyland® Resort **36**

Catalina Island **42**

The Top 10 of Everything

Moments in History **46**

Architectural Landmarks............**48**

Beaches.......................................**50**

Parks and Gardens......................**52**

Places to See and Be Seen **54**

Off the Beaten Path **56**

Children's Attractions.................**58**

Hollywood Connections...............**60**

Movie Theaters............................**62**

Performing Arts Venues..............**64**

Restaurants..................................**66**

Shopping Streets **68**

Los Angeles for Free **70**

Drives and Day Trips...................**72**

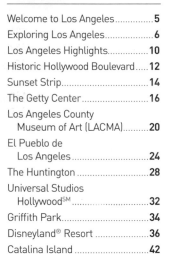

CONTENTS

Los Angeles Area by Area

Downtown..................................**76**

Around Downtown **84**

Pasadena....................................**90**

Hollywood...................................**98**

West Hollywood
    and Midtown..........................**106**

Beverly Hills, Westwood,
    and Bel-Air............................**114**

Santa Monica Bay **120**

Coastal Orange County...............**128**

Streetsmart

Getting To and Around
    Los Angeles...........................**136**

Practical Information................**138**

Places to Stay............................**144**

General Index.............................**152**

Acknowledgments **159**

Within each Top 10 list in this book, no hierarchy of quality or popularity is implied. All 10 are, in the editor's opinion, of roughly equal merit.

Throughout this book, floors are referred to in accordance with American usage; i.e., the "first floor" is at ground level.

Title page, front cover and spine Cars parked along Hollywood Boulevard
Back cover, clockwise from top left
Hollywood Walk of Fame; sunset at Santa Monica Pier; palm trees in Downtown Los Angeles; Hollywood Boulevard; aerial view of Huntington Pier

Welcome to
Los Angeles

City of Angels. City of Dreams. City streets lined with palm trees under a dazzling blue sky. Convertibles cruising the Pacific Coast Highway. Surfers riding a perfect wave. Movie stars leading mythological lives in designer gowns. Beneath this image lies a vibrant, multicultural city for all to enjoy, and with Eyewitness Top 10 Los Angeles, it's yours to explore.

Never would the Spanish founders of the pueblo in 1781 have envisioned that it would one day become a vast urban sprawl, home to over 18 million people from 140 countries. It's a city that dictates culture to the world, yet where no single culture predominates. Stroll down any street and you can hear a dozen different languages and sample the food of a dozen different cuisines. Explore **Pasadena**, with its European style; **Beverly Hills**, where excess is an art form; and **Venice Beach**, with its hedonistic, anything-goes boardwalk.

In an area known for its stars, the **Getty Center**, the **Huntington**, and the **Los Angeles County Museum of Art (LACMA)** are stars among a cultural galaxy. Some of the world's most cutting-edge architecture is rising from Downtown's streets. And, if there's a certain sense of familiarity, look around carefully – you may have seen it in a movie. Free-spirited at heart, this is a city of optimism and possibility.

Whether you're coming for a weekend or a week, our Top 10 guide brings together the best of everything that Los Angeles has to offer, from iconic places such as **Hollywood** to the amazing **Disneyland® Resort**. The guide has useful tips throughout, from seeking out what's free to avoiding the crowds, plus ten easy-to-follow itineraries designed to tie together a clutch of sights in a short space of time. Add inspiring photography and detailed maps, and you've got the essential pocket-sized travel companion. **Enjoy the book, and enjoy Los Angeles**.

Clockwise from top: **Los Angeles skyline, Walt Disney Concert Hall, North Vista at the Huntington, Rodeo Drive sign, A Los Angeles beach with colorful beach houses, West Coaster at Santa Monica Pier, Street performer on Hollywood's Walk of Fame**

Exploring Los Angeles

From the pier of Santa Monica overlooking the Pacific to the star-lined streets of Hollywood, this vast area presents a carousel of activities. Angelinos excel in having fun, whether it's at the beaches, the museums, or the world-famous amusement parks. These two- and four-day itineraries will help you make the most of your time in Los Angeles.

The Hollywood Sign makes for an iconic sight high on the hillside above the city.

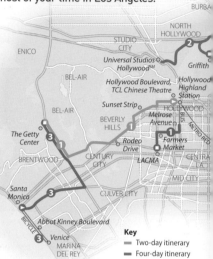

Key

— Two-day itinerary
— Four-day itinerary

Two Days in Los Angeles

Day ❶

MORNING

Start the day on **Historic Hollywood Boulevard** *(see pp12–13)*, at the **TCL Chinese Theatre** *(see p63)*, where you can step among the footprints of the stars. From the Hollywood & Highland Center, spot the famous **Hollywood Sign** *(see p99)*. Then drive past the sights of **Sunset Strip** *(see pp14–15)*. Continue into Beverly Hills for lunch on **Rodeo Drive** *(see p68)*.

AFTERNOON

Head to **The Getty Center** *(see pp16–19)*, a masterpiece of the LA community – wandering through the Impressionist Room or the gardens, while taking in the fabulous views of the coastline and hills.

Day ❷

MORNING

Enjoy breakfast at **Marston's** *(see p97)* in Pasadena before heading over to **The Huntington** *(see pp28–31)*. Pick a couple of gardens to focus on – like the Desert Garden or Rose Garden – and then step into the art gallery to view the masterpieces on display.

AFTERNOON

Take the Metro to Union Station, Downtown. Cross the street to **El Pueblo de Los Angeles** *(see pp24–25)* and have lunch on Olvera Street. From Alameda Street, take the DASH B bus to the striking **Cathedral of Our Lady of Angels** *(see p78)*. Walk down South Grand Avenue to the **Walt Disney Concert Hall** *(see p78)*, **MOCA** *(see p78)*, and **The Broad** museum *(see p80)*.

Four Days in Los Angeles

Day ❶

MORNING

After breakfast at Downtown's **Grand Central Market** (see p79), cross Broadway and look inside the **Bradbury Building** (see p49). Walk over to South Grand Avenue to admire **The Broad** museum (see p80) and the **Walt Disney Concert Hall** (see p78). Take DASH B bus to **El Pueblo de Los Angeles** (see pp24–25) and explore LA's early history. From Union Station, take the Metro to Hollywood/Highland Station.

AFTERNOON

Try a little star-gazing on **Historic Hollywood Boulevard** (see pp12–13) before taking a bus or taxi down to **Melrose Avenue** (see p68) for shopping. Have lunch here or at the **Farmers Market** (see p107) on Fairfax Avenue. Enjoy some of LA's finest art and culture over at **LACMA** (see pp20–23), a few blocks away.

Day ❷

MORNING

Spend the morning among the roses at the **Huntington** (see pp28–31) before driving over to **Universal Studios Hollywood**ˢᴹ (see pp32–3).

AFTERNOON

Focus on the most popular attractions, such as the famed Wizarding World of Harry Potter, King Kong, and Jurassic Park. Then head over to **Griffith Park** (see pp34–5).

Day ❸

MORNING

Pedal a rental bicycle from Santa Monica to Venice along the famous **Venice Boardwalk** (see p122). Snack like a local at **Jody Maroni's** (see p124). Return along **Abbot Kinney Boulevard** and **Main Street** (see p69).

AFTERNOON

Enjoy a blissful afternoon at **The Getty Center** (see pp16–19).

Day ❹

MORNING

Disneyland® Resort and **California Adventure®** (see pp36–41) really require a full day. Buy a Park Hopper ticket that allows entry into both parks. Spend the morning on the rides at **Disneyland®**.

AFTERNOON

Shift over to California Adventure® by late afternoon and be sure to stay for the spectacular World of Color display at night.

Universal Studios Hollywoodˢᴹ is packed with entertaining rides.

Top 10 Los Angeles Highlights

The impressive auditorium
at the TCL Chinese Theatre

Historic Hollywood Boulevard	12	The Huntington	28
Sunset Strip	14	Universal Studios Hollywood℠	32
The Getty Center	16	Griffith Park	34
Los Angeles County Museum of Art (LACMA)	20	Disneyland® Resort	36
El Pueblo de Los Angeles	24	Catalina Island	42

🔟 Los Angeles Highlights

The myth, the velocity, the edginess in creative and technological fields – this is Los Angeles. In just over 200 years, LA has grown from a dusty Spanish outpost into one of the world's largest and most complex cities offering top venues for everything from archaeology and the arts to food. The birthplace of Mickey Mouse and Hollywood, LA has shaped the imaginations of millions.

1 Historic Hollywood Boulevard

The boulevard that gave birth to the movie industry is still associated with the stars, even if the only ones around today are embedded in the sidewalk *(see pp12–13)*.

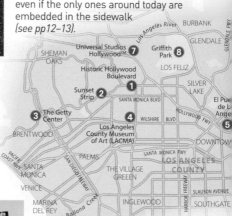

2 Sunset Strip

The heady mix of hip restaurants, nightclubs, and bars along the city's entertainment mile attracts legions of the young and the trendy *(see pp14–15)*.

3 The Getty Center

One of the best bargains in town, this striking hilltop complex is a mecca for fans of European art. Stunning views *(see pp16–19)*.

4 Los Angeles County Museum of Art (LACMA)

One of America's largest art museums, LACMA offers a survey of art from prehistoric times to the present *(see pp20–23)*.

5 El Pueblo de Los Angeles

This historic district preserves LA's oldest buildings, celebrating its Hispanic past with stores, eateries, and festivals *(see pp24–5)*.

The Huntington
6 One of LA's great cultural treasures invites visitors to experience its fine paintings, rare manuscripts, and gorgeous gardens (see pp28–31).

Universal Studios Hollywood^{SM} **7**

A day at Universal involves high-tech thrill rides, live action shows, and special-effects extravaganzas. The Studio Tour takes visitors to the backlot of the working movie studio (see pp32–3).

Griffith Park
8 The largest city park in the nation offers a unique combination of rugged wilderness and such diversions as museums, a zoo, and an observatory (see pp34–5). The Hollywood Sign is here too.

Disneyland® Resort
9 As timeless as Mickey Mouse himself, the original Disney park hasn't lost its magic more than 60 years after it opened (see pp36–41).

Catalina Island
10 This island is a quick and easy getaway, whose considerable charms include crystal-clear waters, miles of undeveloped back country, and a sense of being far away from the bustle of big city LA (see pp42–3).

⭐ Historic Hollywood Boulevard

Hollywood Boulevard, home of the Walk of Fame, has always been synonymous with the glamour of moviemaking, especially in the 1920s and 1930s. But it eventually fell out of favor, teeming with drug addicts and prostitutes. Now the heart of Tinseltown is finally cleaning up its act – the old movie palaces have received facelifts, the Hollywood & Highland complex is a major draw, and even "Oscar" has found a permanent home here.

1 Walk of Fame

Elvis, Lassie, and over 2,600 other celebs have been immortalized with terrazzo and brass stars in the sidewalk **(below)**. A few "special" stars, such as those for the Apollo 11 astronauts, are also installed nearby.

3 TCL Chinese Theatre IMAX

The world's most famous movie theater **(above)** opened in 1927 (see p63) with a screening of Cecil B. DeMille's *King of Kings*. About 200 stars have left their hand- and foot-prints here, and Betty Grable even left prints of her famous legs.

5 The Hollywood Roosevelt

Douglas Fairbanks Sr. presided over the first Academy Awards at this historic hotel **(below)** in 1929, and Marilyn Monroe shot her first commercial by the pool (see p145), later adorned with blue squiggles by the artist David Hockney.

2 The Musso & Frank Grill

During Hollywood's Golden Years, this was the haunt (see p103) of stars such as Clark Gable and the Marx Brothers. Opened in 1919, it is the oldest restaurant in Hollywood and much of its classic interior still remains unchanged.

4 Pantages Theatre

The grande dame of Tinseltown theaters (see p64) sparkles once again in all its restored Art Deco glory. The lobby leads to the magnificent auditorium with its elaborate ceiling. It now hosts blockbuster Broadway shows.

8 Hollywood & Highland

This cornerstone of Hollywood revitalization and mega-entertainment complex **(left)** combines shops, restaurants, night clubs, movie theaters, a hotel, and the 3,400-seat Dolby Theatre *(see p65)*, home of the Oscars.

A STAR FOR THE STARS

A star on the Walk of Fame requires the prior approval of a screening committee appointed by the Hollywood Chamber of Commerce. Of the 200 applications received every year, only 10 percent get the nod – and the privilege to pay the $40,000 fee for installation and maintenance. Studios – and sometimes fan clubs – usually foot the bill. Induction ceremonies are held once or twice a month and are open to the public. Check out www.walkoffame.com to see who's up next.

NEED TO KNOW

MAP P2 ■ Stretches from La Brea Blvd to Vine St

Walk of Fame: Hollywood Blvd between Gower St & La Brea Ave, and Vine St between Yucca Ave & Sunset Blvd

Hollywood & Highland: 6801 Hollywood Blvd

Capitol Records Tower: 1750 N Vine St

Hollywood Museum: 1660 Highland Ave

■ For made-to-order hot churros, go to Street Churros inside Hollywood & Highland.

■ Red signs along the boulevard indicate places the stars used to hang out in.

■ The visitor center at Hollywood & Highland is open 9am–10pm Mon–Sat and 10am–7pm Sun.

Map of Historic Hollywood Boulevard

6 The Egyptian Theatre

Owned by the nonprofit American Cinematheque, this theater *(see p62)* is the birthplace of the "Hollywood premiere".

7 Capitol Records Tower

Once the headquarters of Capitol Records, the world's first circular office building looks like a pile of records with a stylus blinking out "Hollywood" in Morse code.

9 Hollywood Museum

The historic Art Deco Max Factor building showcases a hundred years of film costumes, props, and memorabilia.

10 El Capitan Theatre

The strikingly ornate El Capitan *(see p63)* was Hollywood's first live theater and began screening films in 1941. Today, it is a Disney first-run movie theater.

🔟⭐ Sunset Strip

Sunset Strip has been a haven of hedonism since Prohibition days. Wedged between Hollywood and Beverly Hills, this 1.7 miles (2.7 km) of the Sunset Boulevard is crammed with hot nightclubs, hip rock venues, and fashionable boutiques. During Hollywood's Glamour Age (1930–50), the stars trysted at the Chateau Marmont, partied at Trocadero, and talked shop at Schwab's Pharmacy. Today's hot spots rub shoulders with some historical landmarks.

1 Sunset Plaza

This two-block stretch is lined with European-style restaurants and designer shops teeming with fashionable crowds. Its appeal with celebrities makes it prime territory for star-spotting.

3 Giant Billboards

A testimony to the Strip's unabashed commercialism, these **(right)** mega-sized billboards promote movies, records, products, and even individual stars.

2 Andaz West Hollywood

Formerly known as the "Riot Hyatt," this hotel **(above)** is part of rock history as party central for British bands in the 1960s and 1970s. Led Zeppelin cruised down the halls on motorcycles.

Map of Sunset Strip

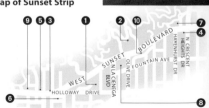

NEED TO KNOW

MAP L3 ■ Along Sunset Blvd between Crescent Heights Blvd & Doheny Dr

Site of Schwab's Pharmacy: 8024 Sunset Blvd

Sunset Strip Tattoo: 7524 W Sunset Blvd

Sunset Plaza: 8600 & 8700 Sunset Blvd

Andaz West Hollywood: 8401 Sunset Blvd

Rainbow Bar & Grill: 9015 Sunset Blvd

■ For killer views and classic American cuisine, head to the new Ivory on Sunset *(see p146)* inside the Mondrian Hotel.

■ Entry to the trendiest venues is easiest around 9pm and on weeknights.

■ Avoid the traffic on the Strip on Friday and Saturday nights.

6 Viper Room

Actor River Phoenix died outside this *(see p112)* club **(left)**, once owned by Johnny Depp *(see p54)* in 1993. Few remember its earlier incarnation as the Melody Room, a favorite with Bugsy Siegel and his mobster pals.

SUNSET BOULEVARD

Sunset Strip takes up only a small portion of the 25-mile (40-km) Sunset Boulevard. Following the path of an old Indian Trail, this major cross-town artery is a microcosm of the cultural, ethnic, and social cauldron that is LA. Starting at El Pueblo in Downtown, it travels west through different neighborhoods, before spilling into the Pacific.

8 Sunset Strip Tattoo

Julia Roberts got a Japanese symbol and Nicolas Cage a stingray at this tattoo studio whose clientele also includes Ben Affleck.

9 Rainbow Bar & Grill

This rock'n'roll bar fills with long-haired rockers and their hangers-on every night. When it was still the Villa Nova restaurant, Marilyn Monroe met Joe DiMaggio on a blind date.

4 Site of Schwab's Pharmacy

In the 1930s and 1940s, Schwab's Pharmacy was a hip hangout frequented by Charlie Chaplin and James Dean. It was torn down in 1988.

5 Whisky a Go-Go

A Strip fixture since 1963, the Whisky *(see p112)* gave the world go-go dancing and The Doors, its house band in 1966. Other stars such as Jimi Hendrix and Janis Joplin also played here.

7 Chateau Marmont

This 1927 hotel **(below)**, has hosted celebrities such as Humphrey Bogart and Mick Jagger *(see p54)*. Howard Hughes ogled at girls by the pool *(see p145)*, and an over-dosed John Belushi made his dramatic exit in 1982.

10 Sunset Tower Hotel

This Art Deco gem *(see p146)*, formerly known as the Argyle, opened in 1931 and has been the home of many a star. Its bar remains a hot address today.

TOP 10 ⭐ The Getty Center

A spectacular art collection, superb architecture, and lovely gardens combine with a hilltop location to create one of LA's finest cultural destinations. Designed by Richard Meier, the Getty Center opened in December 1997 after 14 years of planning and construction. It unites the entities of the Getty Trust created by oil tycoon J. Paul Getty (1892–1976), including research and conservation institutes. At its core is the museum, with its exquisite European art from illuminated manuscripts to contemporary photography.

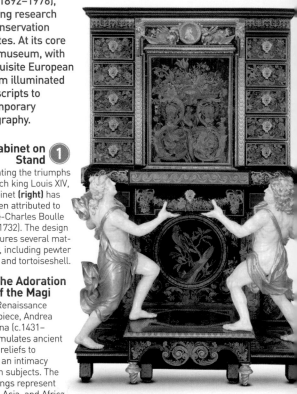

Cabinet on Stand ①

Celebrating the triumphs of French king Louis XIV, this cabinet **(right)** has been attributed to André-Charles Boulle (1642–1732). The design features several materials, including pewter and tortoiseshell.

② The Adoration of the Magi

In this Renaissance masterpiece, Andrea Mantegna (c.1431–1506) emulates ancient Roman reliefs to achieve an intimacy between subjects. The three kings represent Europe, Asia, and Africa.

③ Irises

Dutchman Vincent Van Gogh (1853–90) painted this detailed work **(left)** in the last year of his life in a mental asylum. The intense color and energetic composition borrow from Gauguin and Japanese printmaker Hokusai.

7 The Abduction of Europa

Rembrandt (1606–69) found great inspiration in Ovid's *Metamorphoses*. This work captures Jupiter, disguised as a white bull, spiriting away the princess Europa across the oceans.

8 The Calydonian Boar Hunt

Rubens's (1577–1640) dynamic interpretation of the slaying of the Calydonian boar was painted in 1611. The work established the theme of the epic combat between man and animal.

GETTY VILLA

In a separate location on the Pacific Coast Highway, this museum and educational center is set in a re-creation of an ancient Roman country house and houses over 44,000 Greek, Roman, and Etruscan antiquities dating from 6,500 BC to AD 400. Among the 1,200 items on display are sculptures, everyday artifacts, and treasures such as Cycladic figures. Five of the museum's 28 galleries are devoted to changing exhibitions.

4 Young Italian Woman at a Table

This emotionally charged painting **(above)** by Cézanne (1839–1906) shows off his great versatility and technical ability.

5 Wheatstacks, Snow Effect, Morning

This is one of 30 works that Monet (1840–1926) painted between 1890 and 1891. Set against a soft sky and faintly visible houses, the wheatstacks form a solid, imposing presence in the picture.

6 Albert Cahen d'Anvers

Pierre-August Renoir painted this portrait of composer Cahen d'Anvers in 1881 while deciding to take up commissioned portraiture professionally.

9 Modern Rome, Campo Vaccino

Joseph Turner's view of Rome from the Capitoline Hill **(above)** is the last of his Roman paintings. It shows why this English artist (1775–1851) was celebrated as the "painter of light".

10 Christ's Entry into Brussels in 1889

Belgian James Ensor's (1860–1949) painting is one of the most controversial works of the 19th century. The grotesque scene reflects the artist's uneasiness with society.

NEED TO KNOW

MAP C2

Getty Center: 1200 Getty Center Dr, Brentwood; 310-440-7300; open 10am–5:30pm Tue–Sun (until 9pm Sat); www.getty.edu; parking $15 ($10 after 3pm)

Getty Villa: 17985 Pacific Coast Highway; 310-440-7300; open 10am–5pm Wed–Mon; advance timed ticket required; parking $15 ($10 after 3pm)

■ Picnic in the gardens or courtyard, or buy a light meal at a kiosk or the self-service café.

For gourmet meals, book at The Restaurant.

■ The Getty welcomes kids, with special child-oriented audio guides and a staffed Family Room with games and various hands-on activities.

■ Free architecture and garden tours are offered.

Top 10 Features of the Getty

Water feature in the Central Garden

1 Central Garden
These beautiful – and constantly changing – gardens were designed by visual artist Robert Irwin (b.1928). Wander along tree-lined paths and across a gentle stream to a reflecting pool with floating azaleas and ringed by beautiful specialty gardens.

2 Electric Tram
The Getty experience kicks off with a smooth five-minute ride up the hill from the entrance gate to the Arrival Plaza in a driverless, computer-operated tram.

3 Panoramic Views
On clear days, the views from the Getty's hilltop perch are spectacular, especially around sunset. Take in the vastness of LA's labyrinthine streets, the skyscrapers of Downtown, the Santa Monica Mountains, and the Pacific Ocean.

4 Illuminated Manuscripts
Shown on a rotating basis, the Getty's collection of illuminated manuscripts covers the entire Middle Ages and Renaissance. *The Stammheim Missal* (1120) from Germany is among the most prized.

The Stammheim Missal

5 Drawings
Highlights of this collection, dating from the 14th to the 19th centuries, include Albrecht Dürer's exquisite *The Stag Beetle* (1505) and da Vinci's *Studies for the Christ Child with Lamb* (c.1503–6).

6 Shopping and Dining
There are plenty of options for a day-long visit, including the Museum Store and shops devoted to Impressionism, photography, and the latest exhibits. For refreshments, try the restaurant, café, kiosks, or gourmet picnics.

7 Decorative Arts
The Getty's famous collection of French decorative art and furniture from the 17th and 18th centuries is displayed in a series of period rooms. The paneled Régence salon from 1710 is a must-see.

8 Photography
Known for its images from the early 1840s, the collection concentrates on work by European and American artists. Man Ray's *Tears* is among the most famous pieces.

9 European Painting
Paintings from the Italian Renaissance and Baroque periods, as well as French Impressionism, are particularly well represented.

10 Outdoor Sculpture
Works by many of the 20th century's greatest sculptors are displayed throughout the grounds. The sculptures, including work by Henry Moore, Alberto Giacometti, and Joan Miró, were donated by the late producer Ray Stark and his wife, Fran.

THE ARCHITECTURE

Roosting on its hilltop site on the edge of the Santa Monica Mountains, the Getty Center is an imposing presence, far removed from city noise and bustle. An amazing feat of architecture and engineering, it was designed by New York-based Modernist Richard Meier (b. 1934), an internationally acclaimed architect who also drafted the Paley Center for Media in Beverly Hills *(see p116)*. For the Getty, Meier arranged the main buildings along two natural ridges connected by creative landscaping. Curvilinear elements, such as in the Museum Entrance Hall, combine with angular structures to create an effect of fluidity and openness. This is further enhanced by the use of travertine, a honey-colored, fossil-textured stone quarried in Italy that covers most buildings.

TOP 10 BUILDING STATISTICS

1. Campus size: 24 acres (10 ha)
2. Campus altitude: 900 ft (275 m)
3. Cost: $1 billion
4. Cubic yards (of earth) moved: 1.5 million
5. Travertine used: 16,000 tons
6. Weight of each travertine block: 250 lb (113 kg)
7. Enameled aluminum panels: 40,000
8. Exterior glass: 164,650 sq ft (15,296 sq m)
9. Number of doors: 3,200
10. Length of tram ride: 0.75 miles (1.2 km)

The Getty's columns and vast scale give it the feel of a modern – and thoroughly American – Acropolis.

The Getty Center is distinctive for Meier's curvilinear architecture.

TOP 10 ⭐ Los Angeles County Museum of Art (LACMA)

The largest encyclopedic art museum in the western US, Los Angeles County Museum of Art was founded in 1910 and moved to its present home in 1965. Its vast collection features art from Europe, the Americas, Asia and the Middle East. There is a lively schedule of concerts, lectures, and film screenings, too. In 2010, the Resnick Pavilion was added, a vast open-plan space designed by Renzo Piano that houses rotating exhibitions.

4 Photography and Prints and Drawings

LACMA's photography collection focuses on images produced in the last 60 years, whereas the Prints and Drawings exhibition displays art from the 15th century to the present day.

5 Decorative Arts and Design

This area has European and American decorative design from the Middle Ages to today. The Palevsky Arts and Crafts collection is superb.

1 European Painting and Sculpture

A collection of works **(above)** by Flemish and Dutch masters and French Impressionists, including Monet's *In the Woods at Giverny*.

GALLERY GUIDE

European painting and sculpture, modern art and art of the Pacific are in the Ahmanson Building. The Hammer Building houses Chinese and Korean art, the LACMA store and Children's gallery. The Japanese Art Pavilion is another attraction. The Art of the Americas building is open for research purposes (by appointment). The Broad and Resnick buildings house special exhibitions..

2 Ancient and Islamic Art

LACMA's Art of the Ancient World collection **(right)** spans more than 4,000 years and features horse trappings, stone reliefs, and pottery. The renowned Islamic Art section covers a wide range of art forms.

3 American Art

This collection offers a survey of American art from the 1700s to the 1940s. Among the highlights are works by late 19th-century figurative artists such as Winslow Homer. Other works include paintings by George Bellows and Mary Cassatt, specifically *Mother About to Wash her Sleepy Child*.

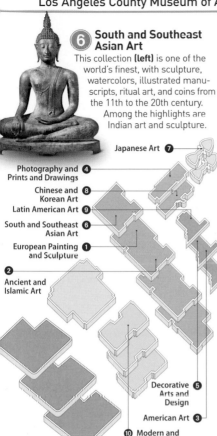

6 South and Southeast Asian Art

This collection **(left)** is one of the world's finest, with sculpture, watercolors, illustrated manuscripts, ritual art, and coins from the 11th to the 20th century. Among the highlights are Indian art and sculpture.

8 Chinese and Korean Art

The largest space devoted to Korean art outside of South Korea has work from the 5th to the 20th century. Chinese works include ceramics, paintings, and bronzes.

9 Latin American Art

These galleries feature ancient American, Spanish colonial, contemporary, and modern works **(below)**. Key pieces range from Mayan works and art by, Orozco, Wifredo Lam, and Torres-Garcia.

Japanese Art **7**

Photography and Prints and Drawings **4**

Chinese and Korean Art **8**

Latin American Art **9**

South and Southeast Asian Art **6**

European Painting and Sculpture **1**

2

Ancient and Islamic Art

Decorative Arts and Design **5**

American Art **3**

10 Modern and Contemporary Art

Floor plan of LACMA

Key to floor plan
- Pavilion for Japanese Art
- Hammer Building
- Art of the Americas Building
- Bing Center
- Ahmanson Building
- Resnick Pavilion
- Broad Contemporary Art Museum
- LACMA West

7 Japanese Art

The Pavilion for Japanese Art is the only building outside Japan devoted to its art. It is closed for retrofitting and will reopen in mid-2020.

10 Modern and Contemporary Art

Matisse, Picasso, and Magritte are among the artists represented in the Modern Art section. The collection here spans from 1945 to now and ranges from paintings to video installations.

NEED TO KNOW

MAP N6 ■ 5905 Wilshire Blvd, Midtown ■ 323-857-6000 ■ www.lacma.org

Open 11am–5pm Mon, Tue, & Thu, 11am–8pm Fri, 10am–7pm Sat & Sun

Adm adults $25; seniors & students $21; free for under-17s; extra charge for special exhibits

■ The LACMA Café serves light meals and refreshments. Ray's and Stark Bar offer farm-to-table dining experience.

■ Free films, Sundays Live musical concerts and free Jazz concerts on Fridays are offered at different times of the year. Check website.

■ Major upgrades to the museum are scheduled. Check website for details.

Top 10 LACMA Masterpieces

1 Portrait of Mrs Edward L. Davis and Her Son, Livingston Davis

John Singer Sargent (1856–1925) was a gifted East Coast society portrait painter. This 1890 work blends loose brushwork (the boy) with stark realism (his mother).

2 Standing Warrior

Standing about 3-ft (1-m) tall, this figure of a king or warrior is the largest-known effigy from western Mexico. It dates from between 200 BC and AD 300.

3 Eagle-Headed Deity

Ancient Syrian palaces were often decorated with intricately carved-stone slabs. This one depicts a deity in the process of fertilizing a tree by scattering pollen from a pail.

Thangka depicting Yama and Yami

5 Yama and Yami

At nearly 2.4-m (8-ft) high, this is one of the largest Tibetan *thangka* paintings outside Tibet. The painting dates from the late 17th to early 18th century and has undergone extensive restoration.

6 Untitled Improvisation III

A pioneer of pure abstract painting, Russian-born Wassily Kandinsky (1866–1944) imbued his canvasses with spirituality expressed through shapes and bold colors, as in this 1914 work.

7 Flower Day

Mexican artist Diego Rivera (1886–1957) is best known for his murals and as Frida Kahlo's husband, but the famous *Flower Day* (1925) shows off his talent as a Cubist-influenced painter.

The Magdalen with the Smoking Flame

4 The Magdalen with the Smoking Flame

French Baroque artist Georges de La Tour (1593–1652) employs deep contrasts between light and shadow to depict his subject with great intimacy and realism.

8 Mulholland Drive

LA-based British artist David Hockney (b.1937) created many panoramic paintings such as this brightly colored and dynamically composed 1980 work, which shows the famous LA road linking the artist's house and studio.

Shiva as the Lord of Dance

9 Shiva as the Lord of Dance

This exquisite sculpture from the 11th century portrays the Hindu god Shiva as the source of cosmic dance, which defines the universe as a continuous cycle of creation, preservation, and destruction.

10 Urban Light

The American sculpture and installation artist Chris Burden (1946–2015) arranged 202 vintage cast-iron street lamps that once resided on the streets of LA into an elegant forest of light and magic that comes to life at sunset.

THE MIRACLE MILE

LACMA sits on a particularly interesting and historic stretch of Wilshire Boulevard. The so-called "Miracle Mile" was the city's first shopping district outside of Downtown and the first ever designed with easy access for the motorized shopper. The man behind this vision was developer A. W. Ross, who, in 1921, bought 18 acres (7 ha) of land between La Brea Boulevard and Fairfax Avenue with the lofty goal of turning it into a "Fifth Avenue of the West." His plan was a wild success, as department stores and upscale retail establishments quickly moved in, but it also marked the beginning of LA's decentralization. By the 1960s, however, a new innovation – the shopping mall – spelled the end of the "miracle." Although a shadow of its former self, the Miracle Mile has been revitalized to some extent, with galleries attracting their share of younger crowds. A few of the Art Deco buildings have survived and are now on the National Register of Historic Places.

**TOP 10
OF ART DECO ON
THE MIRACLE MILE**

1 May Co. Department Store (1940): Wilshire at Fairfax Ave

2 El Rey Theater (1928): 5517 Wilshire Blvd

3 Desmonds Department Store Building (1929): 5514 Wilshire Blvd

4 Commercial Building (1927): 5464 Wilshire Blvd

5 Roman's Food Mart (1935): 5413 Wilshire Blvd

6 Chandler's Shoe Store (1938): Wilshire at Cloverdale Ave

7 Dominguez-Wilshire Blvd (1930): 5410 Wilshire Blvd

8 The Dark Room (1938): 5370 Wilshire Blvd

9 Wilson Building (1930): 5217–31 Wilshire Blvd

10 Security Pacific Bank Building (1929): 5209 Wilshire Blvd

The May Company building is set to house the new Academy Museum of Motion Pictures in 2019.

TOP 10 ⭐ El Pueblo de Los Angeles

This historic district protects LA's oldest structures, all built between 1818 and 1926. Close to the site where 44 Mexican men, women, and children established El Pueblo de Los Angeles in the name of the Spanish crown in 1781, it also reflects the heritage of other ethnic groups that arrived later, including the Chinese, Italians, and French. As LA grew into a metropolis, businesses relocated and the area plunged into deep decline. Now restored, three of El Pueblo de Los Angeles' 27 structures contain museums.

1 América Tropical
Mexican artist David Alfaro Siqueiros's controversial 1932 mural is a visceral allegory about the exploitation of Mexican workers.

2 Blessing of the Animals
Leo Politi's endearing 1978 mural shows the old Mexican tradition of thanking animals for the joy and service they provide humans. Celebrations take place in the Old Plaza each year.

THE MOTHER OF OLVERA STREET

Had it not been for Christine Sterling (1881–1963), an LA socialite-turned-civic activist, the El Pueblo de Los Angeles area may have been completely different. Dismayed by the seediness of LA's oldest neighborhood, Sterling launched her 1926 campaign to save it, backed by *LA Times* publisher Harry Chandler and others. In April 1930, Olvera Street was reincarnated as a busy Mexican market. The Avila Adobe contains an exhibit on her triumph.

3 Old Plaza
Music, dancing, and fun fills the Old Plaza during lively fiestas. It has sculptures of King Carlos III of Spain (1716–88) and Felipe de Neve (1724–84), and a plaque listing the original settlers honors LA's founders.

5 Sepulveda House
Eloisa Sepulveda built this huge 22-room Victorian house in 1887 as her home, a hotel, and two stores.

Olvera Street 4
Named after LA's first county judge, this busy, brick-paved lane has been a Mexican marketplace since 1930 **(right)**. Wander past and try some tacos or *tortas*.

6 Pico House

Pío Pico, the last Mexican governor of California, built this grand edifice **(above)** in 1870. It was LA's first three-story structure and once a hotel.

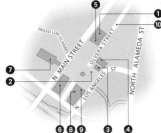

Map of El Pueblo de Los Angeles

9 Old Plaza Firehouse

This two-story brick building is a must-see. Firehouse No.1 with its all-volunteer crew and horse-drawn equipment was operational until 1897. Check out a small exhibit of memorabilia.

10 Avila Adobe

LA's oldest surviving house **(below)**, built by mayor Don Francisco Avila in 1818, went through several incarnations as a military headquarters and boarding house. Today, it contains a visitor center.

7 Plaza Catholic Church

Worshipers have gathered in LA's oldest church **(above)** since 1822. The original was rebuilt in 1861. Features include the painted ceiling and the main altar framed in gold leaf.

8 Chinese American Museum

The Chinese first settled here in the late 19th century. This museum, housed in the 1890s Garnier Building, traces the community's history.

NEED TO KNOW
MAP W3–4

El Pueblo Visitor Center:
Avila Adobe, Olvera Street; 213-628-1274; open 9am–4pm daily; www.elpueblo.lacity.org

Olvera Street market:
open 10am–7pm daily (some shops may open earlier and close later)

Avila Adobe: open 9am–4pm daily

Old Plaza Firehouse: open 10am–3pm daily

Chinese American Museum: 425 N Los Angeles St; open 10am–3pm Tue–Sun; adm $3

■ Olvera Street is great for an authentic Mexican meal. Try the popular Casa Golondrina or the casual La Luz del Día.

■ Volunteer docents offer free guided tours of El Pueblo at 10am, 11am, and noon Tuesday to Saturday. Check in next to the firehouse. The visitor center offers self-guided tour pamphlets.

Following pages Chinese Garden at The Huntington

TOP 10 ★ The Huntington

The Huntington Library, Art Collections, and Botanical Gardens form one of those rare places that manages to please the eye, stimulate the mind, and nourish the soul all at the same time. The former estate of railroad and real-estate baron Henry E. Huntington (1850–1927), it consists of a trio of treasures: the art collections include fine examples of British, French, and American art; the Huntington Library has about seven million rare manuscripts and books, including a Gutenberg Bible; and the Botanical Gardens are a feast of flora in a tranquil parklike setting.

3 Japanese Garden

A place for strolling and quiet contemplation, Huntington's Japanese Garden **(right)** is among the oldest of its kind in the US. Its canyon setting is accented by a waterfall, a shimmering pond filled with *koi* fish and water lilies, and a teahouse.

4 Camellia Garden

Camellias reached the US in the 18th century. With about 1,200 types (in bloom from January to March), this is one of the finest collections.

1 Desert Garden

This exotic garden **(above)**, with its clusters of unusual cacti and flowering succulents, has an otherworldly feel. One of the world's finest, it's a study of the ways in which desert plants adapt to survive in harsh, arid conditions.

5 Chinese Garden

This garden, Liu Fang Yuan, or the Garden of Flowering Fragrance, was inspired by the Chinese tradition of using gardens for scholarly purposes. Pavilions and a teahouse encircle a small lake.

6 North Vista

The palms and statues lining the central lawn of this Baroque garden **(below)** evoke old European palaces. The lawn connects the gallery with a dolphin-studded Italian fountain.

2 Rose Garden

This romantic garden brings you nearly 1,200 rose varieties, some of them with a pedigree going back to ancient Greece. These noble blossoms may be enjoyed from March right through December, but May is the month when most varieties flower.

Gutenberg Bible 7

The Huntington Library's star exhibit, this 1455 Bible (right) is one of only 12 surviving copies printed on vellum by Johannes Gutenberg of Mainz, Germany, the inventor of movable type. The colorful chapter headings and decorations were added by hand.

A SHORT GUIDE

Access the Huntington from either Orlando Road or Oxford Road. Both lead to a large parking lot and from there to the entrance pavilion, where you can pick up a free map. An excellent museum store stocks art books and quality gifts. While you can "do" the Huntington in an hour or two, it's better to come early and spend the day.

NEED TO KNOW

MAP E2 ■ 1151 Oxford Rd, San Marino near Pasadena ■ 626-405-2100 ■ www.huntington.org

Open 10am–5pm Wed–Mon

Adm adults $25 ($29 Sat & Sun); seniors and students $21 ($24 Sat & Sun); children 4–11 $13; under 4s free; free first Thu of month with advance reservation

■ Picnicking is not permitted, but there is an eatery, Dumpling & Noodle House, and a café. Better yet, make reservations (626-683-8131) for English tea served in the Rose Garden Room.

■ Plants from the nursery are available for purchase every second Thursday of the month.

Boone Gallery 8

The Boone Gallery began life in 1911 as Henry Huntington's garage. With columns that echo the Neo-Classical style of the mansion, it is used for temporary exhibitions.

Greene & Greene Exhibit 9

Charles and Henry Greene, known for their houses and fine furnishings, were pioneers of the early 20th-century Craftsman style (see p95).

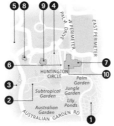

Map of the Huntington

Chaucer's "The Canterbury Tales" 10

This rare 1410 manuscript – known as the "Ellesmere Manuscript" – of English poet Geoffrey Chaucer's most famous work is complete, in fine condition, and filled with luminous illustrations.

Top 10 Huntington Artworks

Pinkie, completed in 1794

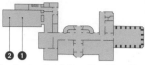

Huntington Art Gallery First Floor Plan

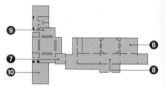

Huntington Art Gallery Second Floor Plan

The Scott Galleries of American Art First Floor Plan

1 Pinkie

Thomas Lawrence (1769–1830) painted Sarah Barrett Moulton, nicknamed "Pinkie," aged 11, in a refreshingly direct and lively manner. She died soon after the painting was completed, possibly of consumption.

2 The Blue Boy

Thomas Gainsborough (1727–88) is one of the most acclaimed British society portrait painters. This famous 1770 painting shows his friend Jonathan Buttall in costume.

3 View on the Stour near Dedham

Romantic landscape painter John Constable (1776–1837) adopted a lyrical approach to depicting nature. His emphasis on sky, light, and other intangible qualities influenced other artists, including the Impressionists.

4 Virgin and Child

A master of early Flemish painting, Rogier van der Weyden (c.1400–64) infused his works with emotional intensity, evident here in the Virgin's face and hands.

5 The Grand Canal, Venice

This 1837 painting is a fine example of the translucency typical of the works of J. M. W. Turner (1775–1851). The tiny person in the lower right corner is Shylock from the play *The Merchant of Venice.*

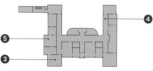

The Long Leg, painted in c.1930

6 The Long Leg

The solitude and anonymity of human existence is a recurring theme in the paintings of Edward Hopper (1882–1967), a leading 20th-century American Realist. Here, these sentiments of loneliness are expressed in a famous sailing scene.

7 Chimborazo

A trip to Ecuador inspired this painting by 19th-century American landscape artist, Frederic Church (1826–1900). Church took creative license when compressing the mountains, desert, and jungle into a single image (1864).

8 Breakfast in Bed

Pennsylvania-born Mary Cassatt (1844–1926) moved to Paris in 1873, where she befriended Edgar Degas and fell under the spell of Impressionism. The subject of mother and child was a favorite.

9 The Western Brothers

John Singleton Copley (1738–1815) was born in Colonial Boston and moved to England just before 1776. This 1783 double portrait is characterized by flowing strokes and strong facial expressions.

10 The Robinson Dining Room

This re-created dining room exemplifies the innovative genius of the brothers Charles and Henry Greene. Designed between 1905 and 1907, it contains original furniture and an amazing chandelier.

HENRY HUNTINGTON'S BIG RED CARS

Henry E. Huntington made his vast fortune by marrying real-estate speculation with public transportation. The largest landowner in Southern California, he established the Pacific Electric Railway in 1901, primarily to get people out to the far-flung new suburbs he was developing. Soon Huntington's fleet of interurban red trolleys – dubbed the "Big Red Cars" – became the world's largest electric-transit system, linking communities across Southern California. By the time he sold most of his holdings to the Southern Pacific Railroad In 1910, the population of LA had tripled to around 310,000. "The last trolley" made its farewell voyage in 1961.

A model of the popular Big Red Car trolleys is one of the highlights of the Huntington collection.

**TOP 10
BIG RED CARS
FACTS AND STATS**

1 Covered four counties

2 Linked 50 communities

3 First ride: 1901

4 Last ride: 1961

5 Track: 1,150 miles (1,850 km)

6 Fleet: 900 cars at peak

7 Passengers: 109 million in 1944 (peak year)

8 Fare: a penny a mile

9 Top speed: 40–50 mph (60–80 km/h)

10 Car length: 50 ft (15 m)

TOP 10 ⭐ Universal Studios Hollywood^{SM}

The world's largest movie and television studio sprang from the imagination of cinema pioneer Carl Laemmle. In 1915, he bought a former chicken ranch, brought in cameras, lights, and actors, and started making silent films. The theme park began taking shape in 1964. Today, Universal Studios Hollywood^{SM} gets more visitors (about seven million a year) than any other attraction in LA County.

① King Kong

The King Kong 360 3-D is the first theme park attraction created by Peter Jackson, who directed the Oscar-winning 2005 film upon which it is based. Guests enter into a world where the film and tram are tied into a simulator that creates a titanic struggle between the 30-ft (9.1-m) tall gorilla and gigantic dinosaurs **(above)**. It is billed as "the largest, most intense 3-D experience on the planet."

② CityWalk

A lively carnival atmosphere reigns along this studio-adjacent promenade with its mix of restaurants, shops, neon signs and entertainment venues.

③ Studio Tour

For a look at movie-making, this 45-minute narrated tram tour **(right)** of the actual working studio is a must. Cruise past 35 soundstages to the vast backlot and outdoor sets.

④ The Simpsons Ride™

Join the Simpsons in the Krustyland theme park as they try to save Bart from Sideshow Bob. The characters are all voiced by the original actors.

5 Jurassic World – The Ride

An upgrade to the previous ride, this **(above)** is part expedition and part thrilling water ride based on the film franchise.

8 DreamWorks Theatre Featuring Kung-Fu Panda

This new multi-sensory experience uses ground-breaking interior projection mapping, 360 degree surround sound and a multitude of special effects on a trip with Master Po and his entourage.

Map of Universal Studios Hollywood℠

6 Revenge of The Mummy℠ – The Ride

The park's first ever roller coaster is a psychological thrill ride that will bring you face to face with the fear of darkness, insects, speed, and heights.

7 Transformers™: The Ride 3-D

Get caught in an intergalactic war between the heroic Autobots and the evil Decepticons in this popular ride.

9 The Wizarding World of Harry Potter

Marvel at the remarkable detail in Hogsmeade village and Hogwarts Castle **(above)**. The 3-D ride, Harry Potter and the Forbidden Journey, and the Flight of the Hippogriff roller coaster will keep you happy.

10 Water World®

For the best stunts, catch this show where the polar ice caps have melted and all land lies beneath the sea. Memorable moments include a crash-landing seaplane and fireballs.

🔟⭐ Griffith Park

Griffith Park is a 6-sq-mile (16-sq-km) natural playground of rugged hills and gentle valleys, draped with native oak trees, manzanita, and sage. As well as hiking and horseback trails, there are picnic areas, golf courses, tennis courts and an outdoor pool. The country's largest urban park owes its existence to the Welshman Griffith Jenkins Griffith (1850–1919). In 1896, Griffith donated a large portion of his estate to the city with the proviso that it become "a place of recreation and rest for the masses."

2 Los Angeles Zoo

Some 1,200 animals are found here *(see p59)*, including koalas and chimps. The breeding program has brought the California condor back from near-extinction.

1 Autry Museum of the American West

This great collection of art and artifacts covers the history and mythology of the American West **(above)**. Star exhibits include a Colt handgun collection.

3 Mount Hollywood Trail

The popular trek to the top of Mount Hollywood, the highest point in Griffith Park, rewards hikers with plenty of exercise and sweeping views of Los Angeles.

JAMES DEAN MEMORIAL

James Dean was one of Hollywood's big stars when, aged 24, he died in a car crash on a lone highway in Central California. A bronze bust outside the Griffith Park Observatory honors the actor, who filmed the famous knife-fight from *Rebel Without a Cause* on the steps of the building. The scene's intensity stems partly from the fact that the actors used real switchblades, though wearing protective vests. The bust is on the west side of the lawn.

4 Travel Town Museum

A fleet of vintage locomotives **(below)**, freight and passenger cars, and several cabooses (goods trains) draw railroad aficionados to this outdoor museum. Children love riding the miniature train.

5 Greek Theatre

A favorite LA outdoor concert venue, the 5,700-seat Greek Theatre *(see p64)* presents a summer season of top musical talent in its leafy natural bowl setting.

6 Forest Lawn Memorial Park – Hollywood Hills

Buster Keaton and Bette Davis are among the celebrities interred in this parklike cemetery dotted with patriotic art and architecture.

7 Griffith Observatory and Planetarium

The observatory (below) has been the park's chief attraction since 1935. A renovation project added 40,000 sq ft (3,716 sq m) of public space.

Map of Griffith Park

8 Merry-Go-Round

A slice of nostalgia in the midst of futuristic LA, this beloved 1926 Spillman carousel has 68 exquisitely carved horses with real horse-hair tails.

9 Bronson Caves

Scenes from *Star Trek*, *Batman*, *Bonanza*, and countless other film and TV productions were shot in this former rock quarry and caves, tucked away in a remote corner of Griffith Park (below).

10 Griffith Park and Southern Railroad

Generations of children have boarded the three miniature trains that chug along a 1-mile (1.6-km) track past pony rides, a Wild West ghost town and a Native American village, moving over a bridge, through a tunnel, past grazing goats and a cactus garden.

NEED TO KNOW

MAP D1

Griffith Park: open 6am–10pm

Griffith Park Ranger Station: 4730 Crystal Springs Dr

Griffith Observatory: 2800 E Observatory Rd; 213-473-0800; open noon–10pm Tue–Fri, 10am–10pm Sat & Sun

Autry Museum of the American West: 4700 Western Heritage Way; open 10am–4pm Tue–Fri, 10am–5pm Sat & Sun; adm

Travel Town Museum: 5200 Zoo Dr; open 10am–4pm daily (to 6pm Sat & Sun)

Bronson Caves: Take Canyon Dr to the end, then take the path past the gate east of the last parking lot

Southern Railroad: open 10am–4:30pm Mon–Fri (to 5pm Sat & Sun)

■ The Crossroads West Café at the Autry Museum of the American West serves breakfast and lunch.

■ Sunset Ranch Stables (3400 Beachwood Dr) leads Friday night horse rides through the park.

🔟⭐ Disneyland® Resort

Since 1955, the landmarks of Disneyland® have been as familiar and as "real" as the Eiffel Tower or the Empire State Building. A second theme park, Disney California Adventure® was been added adjacent to the original in 2001. Downtown Disney®, a further addition, is an entertainment, restaurant, and retail district. The two parks, three Disney hotels, and Downtown Disney® together form Disneyland® Resort.

1 Meeting Mickey

Before meeting Mr. Mouse up close and personal, children are invited to stroll through his house and garden and visit one of his sets. In Mickey's Toontown **(right)**.

2 Haunted Mansion

Dare to enter this mysterious mansion in New Orleans Square inhabited by 999 ghoulish spirits. Board a "Doom Buggy" for a chilling ride.

3 Matterhorn Bobsleds

The park's first roller coaster may look tame but it packs a punch. Strap into a bobsled for a bumpy but exhilarating ride. A must-do for kids!

5 Big Thunder Mountain Railroad

Hop on to this runaway mine train roller coaster in Frontierland for a journey through the Wild West. Charge through bat caverns and brave falling rocks.

6 Roger Rabbit's Car Toon Spin

Get ready for a wild ride in Mickey's Toontown as you pilot a runaway cab through the wacky world of Roger Rabbit.

4 Pirates of the Caribbean

Hold on to your hat as you plunge down into a watery world of darkness **(above)** where wicked pirates plunder the Caribbean.

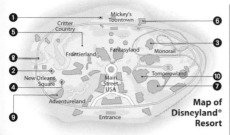

Map of Disneyland® Resort

7 Space Mountain

Soar by comets, stars, and solar systems while plunging into the unknown. Dips and sharp-banked turns will keep you clutching the edge of your rocket ship.

8 Splash Mountain

Follow Brer Rabbit and a cast of other characters from Disney's *Song of the South* on their adventures in Critter Country as you travel along a watery path aboard hollowed-out flume logs.

9 Indiana Jones Adventure™

Join Indy on this bumpy ride through an old temple in Adventureland on a rickety jeep.

Star Tours – Galaxy's Edge 10

This update of one of the park's iconic attractions in Tomorrowland **(right)** features a journey to the Planet Batuu and a visit to the Black Spire Outpost in 3-D.

NEED TO KNOW

MAP F4 ▪ 1313 Harbor Blvd, Anaheim, about 30 miles (48 km) south of LA ▪ 714-781-4565 ▪ www. disneyland.com

Disneyland®: open 8am–10pm Mon–Fri, 8am–11pm or midnight Sat & Sun; adm $109 adult, $95 child (3–9)

Disney California Adventure: open 10am–6pm Mon–Fri, 10am–9pm Sat & Sun; adm $119/$95 for adult/child 3–9

Off-peak Disneyland®: open 9am–6pm Mon–Fri, 9am–8pm Sat & Sun

▪ Try the alfresco Italian at Wine Country Trattoria, within Disney California Adventure®, and Cajun fare at the candle lit Blue Bayou in Disneyland®.

▪ A ParkHopper ticket is a good deal, giving access to both Disneyland and California Dreamin' parks. For an even better deal, get a Southern California CityPASS at citypass.com.

Disneyland® Resort: California Adventure®

1 Pixar Pier

A popular addition to the Disney California Adventure Park, this section features the thrilling Incredicoaster. An Incredibles logo is seen overhead as the guests enter through an archway. Other attractions include Pixar-themed food, the Lamplight Lounge, and more.

2 Mickey's Fun Wheel

You can't miss this enormous, 150-ft- (46-m-) tall Ferris wheel with a grinning Mickey Mouse on the front of it. Two different ride experiences are on offer: the red gondolas on the outer portion of the wheel are fixed – like any normal Ferris wheel – while the other gondolas on the inner part of the wheel swing around freely as they rotate around the wheel. Both give stunning views of Paradise Bay. Be sure to get in the right queue for the nine-minute ride.

3 Animation Academy

For about 15 minutes, a Disney animator gives you step-by-step instructions on drawing your favorite character, such as Mickey, Donald, or Goofy. Materials are supplied. You'll learn a few basic techniques, and you can take home your finished product and frame it for the dining room.

4 It's Tough to Be a Bug!

Starring a cast of termites, stinkbugs, tarantulas, and other creepy crawlies from Disney•Pixar's popular children's film *A Bug's Life*, this 3-D animated movie follows life from a bug's-eye view. The show brims with special effects, some of them rather tactile and intense. Great fun, though not for the squeamish or for small children.

5 Grizzly River Run

Billed as the "world's highest, longest, and fastest," this thrilling

The thrilling Grizzly River Run

Radiator Springs Racers speeding through Ornament Valley

whitewater raft ride takes you on a churning trip through the Sierra Nevada foothills beneath a Grizzly bear-shaped mountaintop. Prepare to get drenched on this one!

6 Toy Story Midway Mania!

Put on your 3-D glasses and be transported to a world of classic American carnival-style games. Shoot darts at balloons, rings at aliens, eggs at barnyard targets, and more. Keep your wits about you and watch out for the special effects!

7 World of Color

A dramatic, whimsical, and dazzling water fountain show, World of Color is spectacular fun for the whole family. Special effects are played out on huge projection screens made from sprayed water, as images from Disney movies and characters run by. Brilliant colors burst, flamethrowers cast waves of flames 50 ft (15 m) into the air, and a musical score fills you with the wonder that is Disney.

8 Guardians of the Galaxy – Mission: BREAKOUT!

Experience the terrifying sensation of free falling in the dark surrounded by audio and visual effects. You'll join the Marvel Comics character, Rocket Raccoon, as he attempts to free other Guardians of the Galaxy figures who are imprisoned in glass display cases suspended over a bottomless pit. Drop sequences with a 'free fall' sensation are part of the fun.

9 Radiator Springs Racers

A smiling six-person convertible takes you on a scenic drive through Ornament Valley before your final preparation for the big race. Once lined up with another car full of guests, the green flag will drop and you'll begin a high-speed, flat-out race through the desert, past camelback hills, red rock formations, geysers, and banked turns.

Soarin' Around the World, the ride

10 Soarin' Around the World

Lift off as you "fly" above the Golden Gate Bridge, the Napa Valley vineyards, the Sierras, and other California landmarks in this virtual hang-gliding adventure. This is the most memorable ride at Disney California Adventure®.

Disneyland® Resort: Practical Tips

E-Ticket Pool at Disneyland® Hotel

① When to Visit

The parks are busiest during the summer, around Easter and Thanksgiving, and again between Christmas and New Year. Crowds thin out from January to March and November to mid-December.

② Beating the Crowds

If you're visiting during peak periods, try to visit midweek instead of weekends and aim to arrive at least half an hour before the gates open, then head for your favorite rides first. Lines are usually shorter at lunchtime and during the parades.

③ Single Lines

If you don't mind riding alone or with a stranger, several attractions in both parks have "single lines" to fill any gaps. Usually these lines are much shorter.

Anna & Elsa's Boutique

④ Kids' Matters

Each park has baby care centers, boutiques and baby stroller rental stations. Some rides have minimum height requirements.

⑤ Parent Swap

Ideal for those travelling with young children. One of your party can wait with the kids while the other rides, and then you can swap, without having to wait in line again.

⑥ Souvenirs

Try not to stock up too early to avoid carrying souvenirs around all day. World of Disney at Downtown Disney® has the best selection.

⑦ Disney Hotels

Staying at one of the three official Disney hotels is not cheap, but they are convenient for access. Disney's Grand Californian (see p149) even has a direct entrance to Disney California Adventure Park®.

Hearthstone Lounge at a Disney Hotel

⑧ What to Bring and What to Wear

Wear comfortable shoes and clothes and bring a hat, sunscreen, and a sweater for the evening, even during the summer. It's all available in the park, but at inflated prices.

⑨ Hidden Mickeys

These can be found hidden throughout the park. People make a game of spotting them.

⑩ FASTPASS System

Insert your admission ticket into machines by select attractions to receive a one-hour time slot for boarding. It's free, but you can only have one FASTPASS active at a time.

WALT DISNEY'S VISION

Mad Tea Party at Disneyland Park

Walt Disney (1901–66), creator of Mickey Mouse, was a pioneer in the field of animation. A relentlessly driven and inventive man, he wished to share his brilliant imagination with families in a non-cinematic way. Watching his own children at play in an ordinary amusement park, Disney was inspired to build a place that was clean and filled with attractions for both parents and kids. Walt Disney envisioned a theme park with five lands: Main Street, a setting plucked from late 19th- and early 20th-century America; exotic Adventureland; Frontierland, paying homage to the Wild West; futuristic Tomorrowland; and Fantasyland, inspired by the song *When You Wish Upon a Star*. Disney picked a 160-acre (65-ha) site in Anaheim and oversaw every aspect of the planning and construction of Disneyland®. When the Magic Kingdom opened its gates in 1955, and 28,000 people stormed in, tears reportedly streamed down Walt Disney's cheeks – his great dream had finally become a reality.

TOP 10
DISNEY BY NUMBERS

1 750 million guests since opening

2 1.1 million plants planted every year

3 Nine US presidents have visited

4 1.2 million gallons of soft drinks sold annually

5 5,000 gallons of paint used each year

6 800 species of saplings throughout the resort

7 30,000 employees ("cast members")

8 4 million hamburgers consumed annually

9 30 tons of trash collected every day

10 100,000 light bulbs illuminate the resort

Walt Disney unveils his plans for Disneyland to a national television audience during the premiere of the television show "Disneyland".

TOP 10 ⭐ Catalina Island

This island may be only 22 miles (35 km) across the sea, but it's a world away from the urban velocity of LA. Ferries dock in Avalon, the island's commercial hub. Most of the interior is a protected nature preserve that may only be explored on foot or bicycle (permit required), or by organized tour. These are excellent ways to learn about the island's history as a destination for sea otter poachers, smugglers, Union soldiers, and mining speculators.

1 Green Pleasure Pier
This green pier has been the hub of Avalon activity since 1909. For years, it was the official weighing station for game-fishing enthusiasts.

2 Lover's Cove
Rent a snorkel and take to the clear blue waters of this poetically named marine preserve teeming with golden Garibaldi (California's state marine fish).

3 Wrigley Memorial and Botanic Gardens
The monument to William Wrigley Jr., built in 1935 with local materials, towers over vast gardens **(below)**. Plants include species unique to the island.

4 Avalon Casino
This Art Deco landmark, built for William Wrigley Jr., opened in 1929 and was never a gambling place. It contains a movie theater and a ballroom that once hosted nationally broadcast concerts. Murals of underwater scenes adorn the exterior.

A WEALTH OF WILDLIFE

Catalina has a unique ecosystem and includes such endemic species as the Channel Island fox and the Catalina ground squirrel. The introduction of non-native animals resulted in overgrazing, a trend the Catalina Island Conservancy is now seeking to reverse. Another restoration project has returned the California bald eagle to the skies. Pelicans, gulls, and cormorants can also be spotted. The ocean waters are abundant with sea lions, Garibaldi, flying fish, and shark.

Map of Catalina Island

5 Casino Point Dive Park

This reserve, set up in 1965, was California's first city-designated water park and is great for divers **(above)**.

8 Two Harbors

Popular with boaters, hikers, and campers, this slow-paced rustic village on a natural isthmus is about 23 miles (37 km) west of Avalon. It is served by ferry from the mainland and by bus from Avalon.

Green Pleasure Pier and Avalon Casino

6 Nature Center at Avalon Canyon

Here, hands-on activities and exhibits showcase the biodiversity of the Island.

7 Catalina Country Club

In 1929, Wrigley Jr. made this the spring training ground of his baseball team. The clubhouse is now a restaurant.

9 Catalina Buffalo

Island explorations may lead to encounters with herds of chocolate-colored buffalo **(right)**. The first 14 animals were brought here in 1924 for a Zane Grey film.

10 Catalina Island Museum

Over 7,000 years of island history come alive here, with artifacts, pottery, and photographs from Catalina's days as the darling of Hollywood.

NEED TO KNOW

Visitors' Bureau: Green Pleasure Pier; 310-510-1520

Wrigley Memorial and Botanic Gardens: www. catalinaconservancy.org; adm

Nature Center at Avalon Canyon: www.catalina conservancy.org

Catalina Island Museum: www.catalinamuseum.org; adm

Catalina Express: 800-613-1212

Island Express: 800-228-2566

Santa Catalina Island Company: 877-778-8322

Catalina Adventure Tours: 877-510-2888

■ Try the Lobster Trap for fresh fish and Steve's Steakhouse for meat.

■ Go swimming, kayaking, snorkeling, or take a glass-bottom boat tour.

■ Catalina is at its best in the evening, after the last ferry has whisked off most of the tourists, so consider an overnight stay.

The Top 10
of Everything

A lifeguard tower on Venice Beach

Moments in History	**46**
Architectural Landmarks	**48**
Beaches	**50**
Parks and Gardens	**52**
Places to See and Be Seen	**54**
Off the Beaten Path	**56**
Children's Attractions	**58**
Hollywood Connections	**60**
Movie Theaters	**62**
Performing Arts Venues	**64**
Restaurants	**66**
Shopping Streets	**68**
Los Angeles for Free	**70**
Drives and Day Trips	**72**

🔟 Moments in History

① 1781: The Founding of Los Angeles

Under orders of King Carlos III of Spain, the governor of California Felipe de Neve laid out a small settlement along a river valley and, on September 4, called it El Pueblo de la Reina de Los Angeles (the Town of the Queen of the Angels) *(see p77)*, another name for the Virgin Mary.

② 1850: LA Becomes a City

After the US-Mexican War (1846–48), Los Angeles became part of the US on April 4, five months before California became the 31st state. With a population of only 1,600, this lawless backwater lacked even such basic urban infrastructures as graded roads and street lights.

③ 1876: The Arrival of the Railroad

Few events have stimulated LA's growth more than its connection to the railroad. A small army of Chinese immigrants built the Southern Pacific track from LA to San Francisco. The last spike – made of gold – was driven in ceremoniously on September 5.

④ 1911: The Movies Come to LA

British immigrants David and William Horsely founded Hollywood's first permanent movie studio, the Nestor Film Company, in an old tavern at the corner of Sunset Boulevard and Gower Street, a site now occupied by a production studio. Within a decade, the district became the world's movie capital, and, by the 1930s and 1940s, Hollywood had officially entered its "Golden Age."

The LA aqueduct in the desert

⑤ 1913: The Opening of the LA Aqueduct

"There it is! Take it!" is how William Mulholland, father of the world's longest aqueduct, famously greeted the first spurt of water to arrive in LA from the Owens Valley, some 250 miles (400 km) north, on November 5. Even today, the LA aqueduct continues to supply over 75 percent of the water needed by the residents of this metropolis, which is partly located in a subtropical desert.

⑥ The 1920s: The Birth of the Aviation Industry

In possession of just $1,000, but driven by a dream, 28-year-old Donald Douglas began designing airplanes in the back of a barber shop. A year later, the first

Donald Douglas and his partner David Davis

Cloudster cargo plane propelled his Douglas Aircraft Company into prominence. It went on to become one of the world's leading commercial airplane manufacturers.

7 1965: The Watts Riots

The arrest of a young black motorist suspected of drunk driving by white policemen on August 11 sparked off six days of rioting and resulted in 34 deaths, over 1,000 injuries, and $40 million in damage.

8 1968: The Assassination of Robert F. Kennedy

On June 5, just minutes after wrapping up a speech to celebrate his victory in the California primary, presidential candidate Robert F. Kennedy was brutally gunned down by Palestine-born Sirhan Sirhan.

9 1992: The LA Riots

Violence erupted again on April 29 after the acquittal of four white police officers on trial for beating up black motorist Rodney King – an incident famously captured on videotape. The toll: 55 dead, 2,300 injured, and $785 million in damage.

Northridge earthquake damage

10 1994: Northridge Earthquake

Millions were jolted awake on January 17 by a violent earthquake measuring 6.7 on the Richter scale. It caused 57 deaths and 6,500 injuries, interrupting water, electrical, and gas services, and damaging freeways and homes.

TOP 10 LA MOVERS AND SHAKERS

Filmmaker D. W. Griffith

1 Junípero Serra (1713–84)
Spanish missionary and founder of 21 California missions, including LA's Mission San Gabriel.

2 Felipe de Neve (1728–84)
The Spanish governor who founded Los Angeles in 1781.

3 Stephen Watts Kearny (1794–1848)
The American general who assisted in the capture of Los Angeles from the Mexican army in 1847.

4 Phineas Banning (1830–85)
The "Father of Los Angeles Harbor," who also constructed Southern California's first railroad in 1869.

5 William Mulholland (1855–1935)
The chief engineer of Los Angeles's Water Department.

6 Edward Doheny (1856–1935)
This miner-turned-multimillionaire discovered oil near Downtown LA and drilled the area's first oil well in 1892.

7 George Freeth (1883–1916)
This Hawaiian-Irish athlete introduced surfing to Southern California in the early 1900s.

8 Harrison Gray Otis (1837–1917)
City booster and publisher of the *Los Angeles Times* for three decades.

9 D. W. Griffith (1875–1948)
Pioneering filmmaker and co-founder of United Artists with Charlie Chaplin, Mary Pickford, and Douglas Fairbanks.

10 Tom Bradley (1917–98)
LA's first African-American mayor governed for an unprecedented five terms – from 1973 to 1993.

TOP 10 Architectural Landmarks

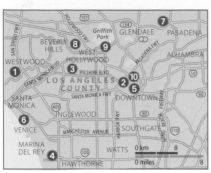

3 Schindler House

MAP M4 ▪ 835 N Kings Rd, West Hollywood ▪ 323-651-1510 ▪ Open 11am–6pm Wed–Sun ▪ Adm

The once-private home and studio of Vienna-born architect Rudolf Schindler (1887–1953) is a modern architectural classic. Completed in 1922, the house has a flat roof, open floor plan, ample use of glass, and rooms opening to a courtyard. It greatly influenced California architecture and today, it houses the MAK Center for Arts and Architecture, which hosts a year-round schedule of architectural tours, exhibitions, lectures, and other interesting events.

1 The Getty Center

The architecture of the extraordinary Getty Center (see pp16–19) is said to outshine the art displayed within its galleries. Architect Richard Meier created an elegant, sophisticated space that is nevertheless warmly welcoming.

2 Walt Disney Concert Hall

This Frank Gehry-designed (see p64) Downtown extravaganza is easily recognized by its shiny and dyna-mically curved exterior. Home of the Los Angeles Philharmonic Orchestra (see p78), it seats over 2,000 people. The city-block-sized complex also contains two outdoor amphitheaters.

4 Theme Building at Los Angeles International Airport

Since 1961, a flying saucer has made its home in the center of LAX, its space-themed design offering the promise of an optimistic future. The architectural firm of Pereira and Luckman found inspiration for their design in Southern California's unique Googie style of futurist archi-tecture, inspired by space, cars and jets. In 2018, it became home for Bob Hope's USO for military members.

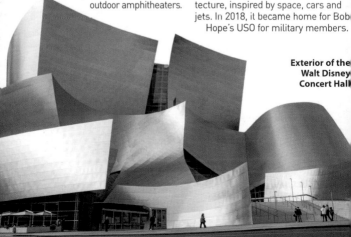

Exterior of the Walt Disney Concert Hall

Bradbury Building atrium

5 Bradbury Building

This light-flooded 1893 office building, with its open-cage elevators, frilly iron work, and marble floors, is one of LA's top architectural landmarks. Architect George Wyman allegedly accepted the job after consulting a Ouija board. Movie buffs might recognize it from *Blade Runner* and *Chinatown*.

6 Chiat/Day Building

MAP B5 ≡ 340 Main St, Venice
≡ Not open to public

Reflecting architect Frank Gehry's sculptural approach, this building was commissioned by advertising firm Chiat/Day as its West Coast corporate headquarters in 1991. It has as its center a three-story-tall pair of binoculars by Claes Oldenburg and Coosje van Bruggen, while the rust-colored columns on the right resemble a deconstructed forest.

7 The Gamble House

This stunning Pasadena Craftsman bungalow *(see p95)* marks the pinnacle of the career of Charles and Henry Greene. Built in 1908 as the retirement home of David and Mary Gamble of the Procter & Gamble family, the house has a beautiful garden, wide terraces, and open sleeping porches.

8 Chemosphere

MAP D2 ≡ 776 Torreyson Dr, Hollywood Hills ≡ Not open to the public

John Lautner's bold, often experimental architectural style is perfectly exemplified in this unique private home in the Hollywood Hills. Resembling a flying saucer on a single concrete column, it was built in 1960, the same year President John F. Kennedy launched the challenge to put a man on the moon. The house was featured in Brian de Palma's 1984 movie *Body Double*.

9 Hollyhock House

One of Frank Lloyd Wright's masterpieces of avant-garde architecture, the 1921 Hollyhock House *(see p101)* was the architect's first LA commission. Anchoring Barnsdall Art Park, the house takes full advantage of the mild California climate. Wright created seamless transitions between indoor and outdoor space and made ample use of patios, porches, and rooftop terraces.

Hollyhock House entrance

10 Cathedral of Our Lady of the Angels

Behind the fortress-like exterior of the cathedral *(see p78)*, designed by José Rafael Moneo, awaits a minimalist hall of worship, where the lack of right angles and supporting pillars creates a sense of spacious loftiness. You don't have to be a Roman Catholic to appreciate the lovely tapestries of the nave, depicting dozens of saints.

🔟 Beaches

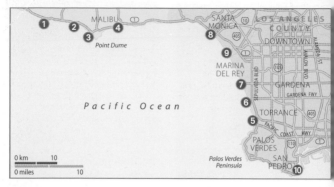

1 Nicholas Canyon Beach
33900 block of Pacific Coast Hwy, near Ventura County Line

This lovely 2-mile (3-km) beach is quieter than most in Malibu because of its isolation and distance from the city. It hugs the base of a bluff and is a great place for those seeking solitude and a tan.

Rock formations at El Matador Beach

2 El Matador Beach
32900 block of Pacific Coast Hwy, Malibu

Rugged, secluded, and dotted with large boulders eroded by nature, this small cliff-backed beach is one of LA's finest. Its remoteness, limited parking, and cumbersome access via a gravelly trail keep the crowds at bay. There are no facilities, but you can explore tide pools and caves, or take a dip. Nude sunbathing is illegal in LA County but some does occur.

3 Zuma Beach
30000 block of Pacific Coast Hwy, Malibu

This 2-mile (3-km) ribbon of fine, sparkling sand is one of LA's most popular beaches. Its clean water and mid-sized waves are great for bodysurfing and swimming. It teems with families on summer Sundays but is nearly deserted the rest of the week, making it perfect for quiet picnics and walks along the beach.

4 Malibu Lagoon State/ Surfrider Beach
MAP A2 ■ 23200 block of Pacific Coast Hwy, Malibu

Wedged in between the Malibu Pier and the gated celebrity enclave, Malibu Colony, this popular beach (see p121) offers many diversions. Watch surfers shred the waves at Surfrider Beach. The eponymous lagoon is a stopover for migratory birds, while the nearby Adamson House with its idyllic gardens overlooks Malibu Pier and Malibu Lagoon.

5 Redondo Beach
MAP D4

A unique horseshoe-shaped pier lined with shops, arcades, and food stands is Rendo Beach's focal point. Rent a paddleboard or kayak and hit the water, or take a bicycle along the cycle path. Boutiques and art galleries are just a few blocks inland.

6 Hermosa Beach
MAP C3 ■ Around Pier Ave

South of Manhattan Beach, Hermosa (see p123) has a busy bar and restaurant scene right where Pier Avenue meets the sand. Beach volleyball is the local pastime and national tournaments take place throughout the year. Only the paved South Bay Bicycle Trail that runs from Marina del Rey to Palos Verdes lies between the sand and private homes.

7 Manhattan Beach
MAP C3 ■ West of Highland Ave

The Beach Boys, who grew up around here, found inspiration for their inimitable surf music in the white sands and glorious waves of this upscale yet relaxed seaside town. Longboarders still compete for the perfect ride, especially around the Manhattan Pier, which is home to the Roundhouse Marine Studies Lab and Aquarium.

8 Santa Monica Beach
MAP A4 ■ Along Pacific Coast Hwy in Santa Monica

This easy-to-access beach (see p59) is one of LA's busiest. Families love the Santa Monica Pier (see p121) with its pretty historical carousel and amusement park. Fitness buffs can get their kicks from pedaling or skating down a paved path running past the restored Muscle Beach, the birthplace of the Southern California exercise craze back in the 1930s.

Ocean Front Walk, Venice Beach

9 Venice Beach
MAP A5 ■ Ocean Front Walk between Venice Blvd & Rose Ave

The beach (see p122) itself plays second fiddle to Venice's outlandish Ocean Front Walk, which is a magnet for eccentrics and those who love watching them. Against a backdrop of trinket shops and cafés, your encounters may include chainsaw jugglers, hulky musclemen, or even a singing Sikh on roller-blades.

10 Cabrillo Beach
MAP D5 ■ Stephen M. White Dr, San Pedro

The sails of windsurfers flutter like giant butterflies along this beach on the breakwater of LA Harbor. Visit the nearby Cabrillo Marine Aquarium to learn about marine life.

Santa Monica Pier and beach

TOP 10 Parks and Gardens

1 Huntington Library, Art Collections, and Botanical Gardens

A perfect synthesis of nature and culture, this amazing estate *(see pp28–31)* houses priceless collections of paintings and rare manuscripts that were started by railroad tycoon Henry E. Huntington and his wife Arabella in the early 19th century.

Fountain at Greystone Mansion

2 Greystone Mansion and Park

MAP J3 ■ 905 Loma Vista Dr, Beverly Hills ■ 310-285-6830 ■ Open most days; call for park hours; mansion open for special events only ■ www.greystonemansion.org

Popular with wedding planners and visitors in search of solitude, this secluded park affords great views of Beverly Hills. Its centerpiece is a 55-room mansion built in 1928 by oil tycoon Edward Doheny as a wedding present for his son Ned. The estate has been featured in many movies, including *Air Force One*.

3 Griffith Park

The country's largest urban park *(see pp34–5)* is filled with museums, entertainment for children, hiking and horse trails, and the famous Griffith Park Observatory.

4 Virginia Robinson Gardens

MAP J4 ■ 1008 Elden Way ■ 310-550-2065 ■ Tours: 10:30am & 11am (1:30pm on select days); call for schedule ■ Adm ■ www.robinsongardens.org

The 1911 estate of department-store heiress Virginia Robinson is one of the oldest in Beverly Hills. Stroll in gardens with fountains and statuettes past towering king palms and elegant camellias flourishing in this quiet hideaway.

5 Exposition Park Rose Garden

MAP D2 ■ 701 State Dr ■ 9am–sunset daily (closed Jan 1–Mar 15) ■ www.laparks.org/exporosegarden/rosegarden.htm

This lovely rose garden dates back to 1928 and features about 15,000 rose bushes that bloom from March through November. Great for picnics or for a respite from museums.

6 Wrigley Mansion and Gardens

The winter home of William Wrigley Jr. (of Wrigley's chewing gum) *(see p92)* is backed by a lovely green rose garden and now serves as the headquarters of the Pasadena Tournament of Roses Association.

Windmill at Self-Realization Fellowship Lake Shrine

7 Self-Realization Fellowship Lake Shrine

MAP C2 ■ 17190 Sunset Blvd ■ 310-454-4114 ■ Open 9am–4:30pm Tue–Sat, noon–4:30pm Sun ■ www.lakeshrine.org

Bathed in an ambience of beauty and serenity, this hidden sanctuary was created in 1950 by Paramahansa Yogananda, an Indian-born spiritual leader. Wander over to the shrine to Mahatma Gandhi or the spring-fed lake, meditate inside a re-created 16th-century windmill, or study the Court of Religions that honors all of the world's major faiths.

8 Franklin D. Murphy Sculpture Garden

MAP C2 ■ UCLA campus, Westwood ■ Open daily ■ www.hammer.ucla.edu/collections/detail/collection_id/6

Tucked away in the northeastern corner of the UCLA campus, this delightful little oasis is dotted with 70 sculptures by some of the greatest 19th- and 20th-century European and American artists such as Auguste Rodin and Alexander Calder.

9 Runyon Canyon Park

MAP N1 ■ At the end of Fuller St off Franklin Ave ■ 323-666-5046 ■ Open until sunset (avoid after dark)

Minutes from the Walk of Fame, this small urban park has some moderately difficult trails and a colorful history – the ruins near the Fuller Steet entrance were built in 1930 by opera star John McCormack, and Errol Flynn lived in one of the pool houses in the late 1950s.

10 Palisades Park

MAP A3 ■ Ocean Ave between Santa Monica Pier & San Vincente Blvd ■ Open daily

Famous for its swaying palm trees and picture-perfect views of Santa Monica Bay (especially at sunset), Palisades Park is a playground for young and old, locals and visitors, families and courting couples. Stretching for 13 blocks atop a bluff overlooking the ocean, the park has benches and lawns that invite picnics and people-watching. A nostalgic curiosity is the Camera Obscura inside the seniors' center at 1450 Ocean Avenue.

Palisades Park

🔟 Places to See and Be Seen

Outdoor seating at The Ivy, a great spot for celeb-spotting

1 The Ivy
MAP L5 ■ 113 N Robertson Blvd, West Hollywood ■ 310-274-8303

The air at this rustic French restaurant is electric with the buzz of Hollywood's power players. Deals are struck daily between movie moguls, celebrities, agents and their high-profile clients. Count yourself very fortunate if you manage to score a table on the fenced-in patio table for some great people- and celebrity-watching.

2 The Viper Room
Celebrities like to hang out with their own kind, and this place (see p15) got its start with Johnny Depp, one of the original owners. It still has enormous cachet, with standing room only for the crowds

The Viper Room entrance

who come to see and be seen (see p112). It's best known as a place to see the freshest, hippest new bands.

3 Fred Segal
Some of the word's most famous stars, such as Rihanna, Jennifer Lawrence, and George Clooney have been spotted browsing for clothes and accessories at this stylish emporium (see p111). It's also a favorite for wardrobe buyers for TV and feature films. The West Hollywood branch is more celebrity-heavy, whereas the Sunset Boulevard branch is another star magnet.

4 Chateau Marmont and Bar Marmont
Celebrities have flocked to this European-style hotel (see p15) like moths to the flame since its opening way back in 1929. Famed for its discretion, it (see p145) has remained a favorite spot for celebrity trysts. Check out the chic Bar Marmont, (see p112).

5 Spago Beverly Hills
The owner of this restaurant, Wolfgang Puck, is as famous as its patrons. The dining room is a popular spot (see p119) where you might run into many celebrities having a great time.

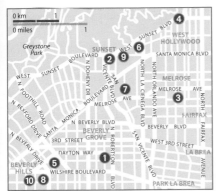

8 Barneys New York

MAP J6 ■ 9570 Wilshire Blvd, Beverly Hills ■ 310-276-4400

Shop till you drop while keeping an eye out for superstars and celebrities at this luxurious LA department store. All the major designers from Armani and Gucci to Helmut Lang and Dolce & Gabbana are represented here. Take in the good views from the outdoor tables in the rooftop deli.

6 Bar 1200

Catering to a "Rolls-Royce" rock'n'roll crowd, this hot hangout at the Sunset Marquis Hotel *(see p147)* was once owned by Rande Gerber, husband of supermodel Cindy Crawford. Getting past the velvet rope isn't easy, especially when big names such as U2's Bono come by.

9 Book Soup

MAP L3 ■ 8818 Sunset Blvd, West Hollywood ■ 310-659-3110, 1-800-764-BOOK (toll free)

This excellent independent bookstore draws a sizeable celebrity contingent with its eclectic offerings, including international publications. Try and increase your chances of meeting a star by attending one of their book readings or book-signing sessions. Call for schedules.

10 LA Lakers Games at Staples Center

The Los Angeles Lakers, the city's fabled basketball team, always attract a fair number of celebrities to their games at the Staples Center. Number One fan, Jack Nicholson, can usually be spotted courtside, and Vanessa Hudgens and Justin Bieber are regulars. Leonardo DiCaprio, Jennifer Lopez, and Ben Affleck have also made appearances.

Bar 1200 at Sunset Marquis Hotel

7 Urth Caffè

MAP L4 ■ 8565 Melrose Ave, West Hollywood ■ 310-659-0628

This West Hollywood eating joint is a health- and waist-conscious café on the celebrity radar, but most days it's just the usual in-crowd munching on vegetarian lasagne and New York cheesecake. The patio offers the best vantage point for checking out the crowd from behind sunglasses.

The massive Staples Center

🔟 Off the Beaten Path

1 Museum of Latin American Art

MAP E4 ▪ 628 Alamitos Ave, Long Beach ▪ 562-437-1689 ▪ Open 11am–5pm Wed–Sun ▪ Adm (free for under 12s) ▪ www.molaa.org

Part of Long Beach's emerging East Village Arts District, this lively museum is the only one in the western United States dedicated to showcasing the modern and contemporary works of Latin American artists. A permanent collection of 1,500 works, travel-ing exhibitions, and a sculpture garden instruct and inspire.

Paintings at Velveteria

2 Velveteria

MAP W5 ▪ 711 New High St, Chinatown ▪ 503-309-9299 ▪ Open 11am–6pm Wed–Mon ▪ www.velvet eria.com

Quirky and fun, this museum has on display hundreds of velvet paintings curated from a collection of nearly 4,000 pieces. While never accepted in the art world as legitimate art, there are serious works here, such as the Polynesian art of Edgar Leetag. Less serious is the Hall of Elvis.

Book tunnel at The Last Bookstore

3 The Last Bookstore

MAP V5 ▪ 453 Spring St ▪ 213-488-0599 ▪ Open 10am–10pm Sun–Thu, 10am–11pm Fri–Sat, 10am–9pm Sun ▪ www.lastbookstorela.com

An abandoned bank has transformed into a world devoted to the love of reading and books as art. It's not just another bookstore, but a Downtown destination where devotees come to explore 250,000 titles, pass through a book tunnel, or wander the adjacent art galleries.

4 Watts Towers

MAP E3 ▪ 1765 E 107th St, Watts ▪ 213-847-4646 ▪ www. wattstowers.org

This folk-art masterpiece is a whimsical trio of spires, adorned with rainbow-colored pieces of tile, glass, pottery, shells, and other scavenged materials. The sculpture, completed in 1954, represents the life's work of Italian immigrant Simon Rodia. The high-crime neigh-borhood is best avoided after dark.

5 Metro Art

Stations throughout the Metro Rail system exhibit delightful murals, sculpture, artwork, and photography reflective of the local neighborhood around the stop. These award-winning installations represent the work of 100 different artists. Be sure to download, or request in advance, the *Art Guide: A Tour of Metro's Artwork* before setting out.

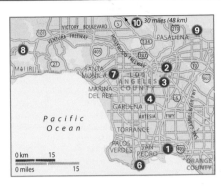

⑥ Los Angeles Maritime Museum

MAP D4 ■ Berth 84, at the foot of 6th St, San Pedro ■ 310-548-7618 ■ Open 10am–5pm Tue–Sun ■ www.lamaritime museum.org

This museum celebrates LA's seafaring tradition through displays of nautical models and memorabilia. A highlight is the exhibit about the USS *Los Angeles*, a navy cruiser that fought in China and the Korean War. Adjacent is the battleship USS *Iowa*, which transported Roosevelt across the Atlantic to meet Winston Churchill during World War II.

⑦ Museum of Jurassic Technology

9341 Venice Blvd, Culver City ■ 310-836-6131 ■ Open 2–8pm Thu, noon–6pm Fri–Sun ■ Adm (free for under 12s) ■ www.mjt.org

The doors of this bizarre yet fun museum open up a parallel universe, where the seemingly mundane becomes extraordinary. A throwback to the natural science museums of the 19th century, exhibits include Cameroonian stink ants and a display of stereo floral radiography.

⑧ Paramount Ranch

2903 Cornell Rd, Agora Hills ■ 805-370-2301 ■ nps.gov

The mountains surrounding LA have provided a natural backdrop for Westerns since the 1920s, and the old buildings of Paramount Ranch have featured in many of the productions. Aside from an occasional film shoot, the ranch is open to explore, as are the adjacent hiking trails of the scenic Santa Monica Mountains National Recreation Area.

⑨ Sierra Madre

MAP F1

Just east of Pasadena, Sierra Madre is the type of old-fashioned town you can't imagine existing in the LA urban landscape. It is home to many of LA's creative artists, and a delightful mix of boutiques and cafés line the town center. Residential streets hold a number of original Craftsman houses. Come in March for the annual Wisteria Festival.

⑩ Vasquez Rocks

10700 Escondido Canyon Rd, Agua Dulce ■ 661-268-0010 ■ www. parks.lacounty.gov

On the National Register of Historic places for its significance in Native American prehistory, this 1.5-sq-mile (3.8-sq-km) natural desert park with its distinctive rock formations has found fame as a film location site for over 100 movie, TV, and music video productions from *Star Trek* to *The Flintstones*. Wear hiking boots and bring along a picnic.

The majestic Vasquez Rocks

🔟 Children's Attractions

1 California Science Center

Located in Exposition Park, this interactive museum *(see p86)* makes science and technology fun. Feel a simulated earthquake, design a car, and marvel at the inner workings of a 50-ft (15-m) long robot named Tess. The adjoining Air and Space Gallery focuses on the principles of flight and space exploration.

Tess at the California Science Center

2 Universal Studios Hollywood℠

This theme park *(see pp32–3)* attached to the world's largest movie studio is LA's biggest tourist attraction. A ticket buys a day of thrill rides and live action shows, and includes encounters with Spider-Man, King Kong, and other movie icons. A must-do is the narrated tram tour to the famous backlot sets.

3 Natural History Museum

This engaging museum *(see p85)* pays homage to the entire animal kingdom, including extinct

species such as the perennially popular dinosaurs. Special child-oriented facilities include the Discovery Center, stocked with puppets, storybooks, and a fossil-rubbing station, and the Insect Zoo, home to a host of creepy crawlies.

4 Cabrillo Marine Aquarium

MAP D5 ■ 3720 Stephen White Drive, San Pedro ■ 310-548-7562 ■ Open noon–5pm Tue–Fri, 10am–5pm Sat & Sun ■ Donation ■ www.cabrillo marineaquarium.org

This facility offers an entertaining introduction to life in Southern California's ocean waters. The playful yet educational exhibits are ideal for children. Activities, include guided tide pool walks, a marine laboratory workshop, and supervised "camp-outs" for kids.

5 Aquarium of the Pacific

MAP E4 ■ 100 Aquarium Way, Long Beach ■ 562-590-3100 ■ Open 9am–6pm daily ■ Adm ■ www. aquariumofpacific.org

Take a virtual dive through three regions of the Pacific Ocean at this aquarium. Explore the kelp beds of Southern California, the stormy shores of the north Pacific, and the coral reefs of the tropical Pacific. "Dive charts" help you identify the species.

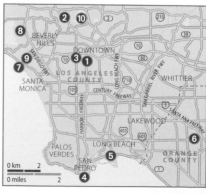

The popular Pacific Park® at the Santa Monica Pier

6 Santa Monica Pier

Pet a sea cucumber, take to the skies in a Ferris wheel, or watch local fisherfolk reel in their latest catch at this pier. These are just some of the activities on California's oldest amusement pier (see p121), whose attractions draw over three million people a year. During summer, a free concert series takes place on Thursday nights.

7 Disneyland®

Over half a century after it first opened its doors, the "magic kingdom" (see pp36–41) continues to be right on top of most children's must-see lists. A one-, two-, or three-day visit is guaranteed to delight, amaze, and exhaust the kids, especially since expansions have added a second theme park, Disney's California Adventure®, and the Downtown Disney® entertainment district to Disneyland®.

8 Getty Center Family Room

Five discovery "coves" highlight different art forms from sculpture to photography (see pp16–19). Children can decorate an illuminated manuscript, build a tube sculpture, or design a mask. A treasure-hunt wall focuses museum works that you can later visit. "Detective cards" allow kids to become active observers once in the galleries.

9 Cayton Children's Museum by ShareWell

MAP K6 ■ 395 Santa Monica Place ■ Open 10am–7pm Mon–Sat, noon–7pm Sun ■ Adm ■ www.cayton museum.org

Located in the Santa Monica Place mall, this new venue features free-form objects, round rooms and an open air plan. Hands-on exhibits include the Courage Climber rope canopy and the Hello Booth with phones powered by imagination.

10 Los Angeles Zoo

MAP D1 ■ 5333 Zoo Drive ■ Open 10am–5pm daily ■ Closed 25 Dec ■ Adm (free for under 2s) ■ www.lazoo.org

The Elephants of Asia exhibit and the Winnick Family Children's Zoo, both are favorites at the LA Zoo. Pet barnyard animals at Muriel's Ranch, greet the baby animals in the nursery, and dress up for interactive play and storytelling at the Adventure Theater.

Queues outside Los Angeles Zoo

🔟 Hollywood Connections

DC Universe: The Exhibit, part of the Warner Bros Tour

1 Warner Bros Tour
MAP D1 ■ 3400 Riverside Dr, Burbank ■ 818-846-1403 ■ Adm ■ www.wbstudiotour.com

This excellent three-hour tour provides a thorough look at both the glamorous history as well as the day-to-day working reality of a major motion picture studio. Watch an introductory movie, visit the museum, and outdoor sets. Tour routes vary.

2 Samuel French Theatre and Film Bookshop
MAP N3 ■ 7623 Sunset Blvd ■ 866-598-8449 ■ www.samuelfrench.com

This purveyor of printed Hollywood material is geared to the needs of professional actors and screenwriters. The company also publishes and leases scripts of live plays.

The Samuel French bookshop

3 Larry Edmunds Bookshop
MAP P2 ■ 6644 Hollywood Blvd ■ 323-463-3273 ■ www.larryedmunds.com

Books about animation, acting, and Hollywood history, as well as historic movie posters, publicity stills, and screenplays – this store has it all.

4 American Cinematheque
To listen to Hollywood actors and directors discuss movies, attend screenings by this group (see p62) at the historic Egyptian Theatre (see p13). The schedule ranges from retrospectives to filmmaker tributes.

5 It's a Wrap!
MAP D1 ■ 3315 W Magnolia Blvd, Burbank ■ 818-567-7366 ■ www.itsawraphollywood.com

Much of the clothing worn by actors ends up here. There are bargains galore, and each item sports a tag identifying the show it appeared on.

6 TMZ Hollywood Tour
MAP P2 ■ 6925 Hollywood Blvd ■ 855-486-9868 ■ Tours: check website for timings ■ Adm ■ www.tmz.com/tour

This two-hour, open-air bus tour is run by the TV show, *TMZ*. Guides are poised to spot celebrities and interview them on the street. An edgy, fast look at current hot star hangouts.

7 Sony Pictures Studio Tour

MAP D2 ▪ 10202 W Washington Blvd, Culver City ▪ 310-244-8687
▪ **Tours: call for schedule, reservations required** ▪ **Adm**

This giant movie lot was the historic home of the famous MGM, producer of well-known classics such as *The Wizard of Oz*, until purchased by Sony in 1990. The two-hour walking tour may include a visit to the set of the game show *Jeopardy*.

8 Paramount Pictures Studio Tour

MAP R4 ▪ 5555 Melrose Ave
▪ 323-956-1777 ▪ **Adm** ▪ www.paramountstudiotour.com

See the famous New York backlot and learn about the history of this working movie studio on a two-hour tour. Reservations required.

Paramount Pictures Studio entrance

9 Margaret Herrick Library

MAP L6 ▪ 333 S La Cienega Blvd, Beverly Hills ▪ 310-247-3000
▪ **Open 10am–6pm Mon, Thu, & Fri, 10am–8pm Tue** ▪ **ID required**

It's easy to get lost in this repository of movie-related books and publications, operated by the Academy of Motion Picture Arts and Sciences.

10 Audiences Unlimited

www.tvtickets.com

A great way to see stars live is to be part of a studio audience. This organization handles the distribution of free tickets to live tapings, mainly of game shows and sitcoms. Book early for the best selection. Tickets are available online 30 days ahead.

TOP 10 LA SCANDALS

Fatty Arbuckle's police headshot

1 Fatty Arbuckle
The silent-era funnyman was charged with the murder of actress Virginia Rappe in 1921, thus ending his career.

2 Errol Flynn
He was charged with statutory rape in 1942.

3 Lana Turner
The actress's mobster lover was found stabbed to death in her house in 1958. Her teenage daughter took the blame.

4 Sharon Tate
Tate, 8½ months pregnant, was among the victims of the Charles Manson murders in 1969.

5 John Belushi
A drug overdose ended this Blues Brother's life at age 33 in 1982 at the Chateau Marmont Hotel.

6 O. J. Simpson
The football star was cleared of the murder of Nicole Brown Simpson and Ron Goldman in 1994.

7 Heidi Fleiss
Fleiss ran an elite call-girl racket and received 37 months in jail in 1997.

8 Bill Cosby
In 2018, he was sentenced to prison for aggravated indecent assault. More than 50 women have accused him of similar sexual misconduct.

9 Hugh Grant
Caught in a sexual act with a prostitute in his car, he was given two years' probation and a fine in 1995.

10 Harvey Weinstein
Weinstein was expelled from the Academy of Motion Pictures and sent to prison in 2018 after more than 80 women accused him of sexual assault and rape.

⒑⓪ Movie Theaters

① Pacific Theatres at The Grove
MAP N5 ■ 189 The Grove Drive, Midtown ■ 323-692-0164

State-of-the-art meets Art Deco charm at this 14-screen complex that evokes the grand theaters of early LA. Great for star sightings.

Pacific Theatres at The Grove

② New Beverly Cinema
MAP P5 ■ 7165 Beverly Blvd ■ 323-938-4038 ■ www.thenew bev.com

Owned by Quentin Tarantino, this historic single-screen theater shows only movies on 35mm and 16mm film, most of which are from his private collection. Significant upgrades in 2018 have refreshed the space.

③ Cinemark 18 & XD
MAP D3 ■ 6081 Center Dr, off Fwy 405 ■ 310-568-3375

This cutting-edge theater has been aptly subtitled "cinema de lux".

Enjoy recently released movies while sitting in large and luxurious leather chairs.

④ ArcLight Cinemas and Cinerama Dome
MAP Q3 ■ 6360 W Sunset Blvd ■ 323-464-4226

The exquisite 15-screen ArcLight is the shiny neighbor of the futuristic Cinerama Dome (see p101). The lobby leads to a lively café-bar with terrace. Good for star sightings.

⑤ The Egyptian Theatre
MAP P2 ■ 6712 Hollywood Blvd ■ 323-466-3456

This oldest of Hollywood Boulevard's themed 1920s movie palaces (see p13) today houses the American Cinematheque. It presents art house fare and the documentary *Forever Hollywood* on weekends.

⑥ California Science Center IMAX Theater
MAP D2 ■ 700 Exposition Park Dr ■ 323-744-7400 ■ www.california sciencecenter.org

IMAX stands for "maximum image" and with a screen that is seven-stories tall and 90-ft (27-m) wide (see p86), it's a fitting name. A six-channel surround-sound system ensures total sensory immersion.

California Science Center IMAX Theater

7 The Nuart Theatre
MAP C2 ■ 11272 Santa Monica Blvd ■ 310-281-8223 ■ www.landmarktheaters.com

One of LA's finest independent theaters, this shows movies that most multiplexes would avoid. The cult classic *The Rocky Horror Picture Show* still runs every Saturday.

8 TCL Chinese Theatre IMAX
MAP P2 ■ 6925 Hollywood Blvd ■ 323-464-6266

This flashy 1927 Chinese fantasy palace *(see p12)* is still the site of movie premieres. Catch a blockbuster here – you may get to sit next to a celebrity. The sixplex next door has none of the original's historic flair.

TCL Chinese Theatre IMAX

9 Bing Theater at LACMA
MAP N6 ■ 5905 Wilshire Blvd, Midtown ■ 323-857-6010

■ www.lacma.org

LA's famous art museum *(see pp20–23)* presents high-brow retrospectives of a particular actor or director in its on-site theater. Catch classic films for cheap on Tuesdays at 1pm.

10 El Capitan Theatre
MAP P2 ■ 6838 Hollywood Blvd ■ 323-467-7674

Old-time Hollywood glamour has returned to LA courtesy of the famed Walt Disney Company, which has restored this 1926 theater *(see p13)*. It now functions as a first-run cinema showing Disney flicks, sometimes preceded by lavish live shows.

TOP 10 OSCAR FACTS

Oscar statue inside Dolby Theatre

1 How the Oscar got its Name
The statuette got its name in 1931 after future Academy executive director Margaret Herrick remarked that it resembled her uncle Oscar.

2 Oscar by Numbers
The 13.5-inch (34-cm) tall, 8.5-lb (3.9-kg) Oscar has been handed to winners more than 3,100 times.

3 Top Four Oscar-winning Films
Ben Hur, Titanic, and *Lord of the Rings: Return of the King* gained 11 awards each. *West Side Story* received ten.

4 Actor with Most Oscars–Male
A tie – Walter Brennan, Daniel Day-Lewis and Jack Nicholson have each won three times.

5 Actor with Most Oscars–Female
Katherine Hepburn, Ingrid Bergman and Meryl Streep are four-time Oscar winners.

6 All-time Oscar Winner
Walt Disney – 26 awards.

7 Youngest Oscar Winner
Shirley Temple, who was six years and 310 days old when she won.

8 Oscar Controversy
In 1972, Marlon Brando refused the Best Actor award in protest against the US government's mistreatment of Native Americans.

9 Oscar Venues
The Hollywood Roosevelt Hotel, Ambassador Hotel, Shrine Auditorium, Pantages Theatre, and The Dolby (current) are the famous ones.

10 Oscar Parties
The official post-award Governor's Ball moved in 2002 to the Hollywood & Highland Grand Ballroom.

🔟 Performing Arts Venues

1 Pantages Theatre
MAP Q2 ■ **6233 Hollywood Blvd** ■ **323-468-1770** ■ **www. hollywoodpantages.com**

This Art Deco jewel *(see p12)* has been restored to its 1929 glory. Once a movie palace, its eye-popping auditorium hosted the Academy Awards from 1949–59.

Walt Disney Concert Hall auditorium

2 Walt Disney Concert Hall

This Frank Gehry creation *(see p48)*, the newest part of the Music Center, features cleverly designed seating that makes listening to the LA Philharmonic Orchestra beneath the sail-like ceiling *(see p78)* an unforgettable experience.

3 Music Center
MAP V4 ■ **135 N Grand Ave, Downtown** ■ **213-972-7211**

This three-venue arts center represents LA culture. The LA Opera, directed by Plácido Domingo, makes its home at the Dorothy Chandler Pavilion, while cutting-edge plays are presented at the Ahmanson Theater and the Mark Taper Forum.

4 Ford Amphitheatre
MAP P1 ■ **2580 Cahuenga Blvd E** ■ **323-461-3673** ■ **www. fordtheatres.org**

Built in 1920 and embraced by the Hollywood Hills, this intimate outdoor amphitheater presents a multicultural program of music, dance, film, and theater.

5 Greek Theatre
MAP D2 ■ **2700 N Vermont Ave** ■ **323-665-5857** ■ **www.greek theatrela.com**

Tucked into a hillside in Griffith Park, the popular Greek Theatre *(see p34)* has featured such musical greats as B. B. King. Stars leave their handprints on the Wall of Fame.

6 Theatricum Botanicum
MAP B2 ■ **1419 N Topanga Canyon Blvd** ■ **310-455-3723** ■ **www.theatricum.com**

This lovely theater venue was the brainchild of Will Geer, best known for his portrayal of Grandpa in the 1970s TV series *The Waltons*. The productions are popular classics.

7 Hollywood Bowl

Concerts beneath the stars at this natural amphitheater *(see p100)* are a summer tradition. The range extends from Beethoven and The Beatles to cabaret and rock. Enjoy a picnic before the show. Cheap tickets are available for some shows.

Fireworks display, Hollywood Bowl

The exterior of the Dolby Theatre

8 Dolby Theatre

MAP P2 ■ 6801 Hollywood Blvd ■ 323-308-6300 ■ Half-hourly tours: 10:30am–4pm daily ■ Adm ■ www.dolbytheatre.com

Home of the Academy Awards since 2002, this is a stunning venue with a five-level lobby and a grand spiral staircase. Dolby 3-D video imaging and advanced audio technology add to the enjoyment.

9 Royce Hall

MAP C2 ■ UCLA Campus, Westwood ■ 310-825-2101 ■ www.cap.ucla.edu

One of UCLA's original buildings, the 1929 Romanesque Royce Hall (see p116) once hosted greats such as George Gershwin. Today, the hall presents an avant-garde calendar of dance, music, and theater events.

10 Microsoft Theater

MAP S6 ■ 777 Chick Hearn Court ■ 213-763-6030 ■ www.microsofttheater.com

This venue presents concerts on the largest indoor stage in Southern California. The theater also hosts awards shows such as the ESPY Awards and the Primetime Emmys.

TOP 10 COMEDY CLUBS

1 HaHa Café
5010 Lankershim Blvd
■ 818 508 4995
This club nurtures budding comics.

2 The Groundlings
7307 Melrose Ave ■ 323-934-4747
TV star Lisa Kudrow (of the TV series *Friends*) graduated from here.

3 The Improv
8162 Melrose Ave ■ 323-651-2583
Robin Williams tickled funny bones at this famous haunt with an eatery.

4 Comedy Union
5040 W. Pico Blvd ■ 323-934-9300
New and established comics perform here with longer sets than most clubs.

5 Comedy Store
8433 Sunset Blvd ■ 323-650-6268
A legendary club that launched the careers of Jim Carrey and Michael Keaton.

6 Upright Citizens Brigade Theatre
5919 Franklin ■ 323-908-8702
Comedians from the training center perform improv and sketch comedy on a small stage in an intimate atmosphere.

7 ACME Comedy Theater
135 N La Brea Ave ■ 323-525-0202
It presents the best troupe for sketch comedy in LA in its own theater.

8 The Comedy & Magic Club
1018 Hermosa Ave, Hermosa Beach
■ 310-372-1193
Famous comics including Jay Leno (on most Sundays) test new material here.

9 The Ice House
24 N Mentor Ave, Pasadena
■ 626-577-1894
It is one of the US's oldest comedy clubs.

10 The Laugh Factory
8001 Sunset Blvd ■ 323-656-1336
It features big name acts and promising newcomers of all ethnic backgrounds.

The Laugh Factory at Sunset Blvd

🔟 Restaurants

Water Grill, with upscale decor and some of the best seafood in LA

1 Water Grill

A premier seafood joint, this *(see p83)* is usually packed with patrons appreciative of the dock-fresh fare and superb service. Chef Jesse Riofir turns each dish into a celebration of bold flavors and pleasing textures. The yummy white clam chouder and hand-cut tuna tartare are outstanding, and the oyster bar scores high with the pre-theater crowd.

boeuf, served table-side, is indicative of the kitchen's lofty aspirations. Try the chef's superb tasting menu. As it is located inside the Walt Disney Concert Hall, it's a favorite for luxury pre-performance dining and special occasions.

Sea urchin, Providence

2 Patina

A long-time darling of food critics and gourmets, Patina is where star chef Joachim Splichal takes his innovative French-Californian cuisine to new heights. The melt-in-your-mouth *côte de*

3 Providence

An LA institution, Providence serves some of the West Coast's best wild-caught, sustainable seafood, fresh from American and inter-national waters. From the series of separate, elegant dining areas, choose the intimate patio room if you are in search of a romantic eve-ning. Fresh truffles are a specialty, as are the changing tasting menus and wine pairings.

4 Echigo

Fine, imaginatively presented sushi of all types is the only offering at this eatery *(see p113)*. The ambience is simple and plain, with only 12 seats at the L-shaped bar and service is attentive. The *omakase* (chef's choice) is outstanding.

⑤ Matsuhisa

This *(see p119)* is the original of a small chain of restaurants serving Nobu Matsuhisa's inspired Japanese-Peruvian fusion fare. The sushi is impeccable and the tempura extra-light, but the chef's talent really lies in cooked seafood dishes, many paired with Nobu's perky sauces. Celebrity sightings are likely. Make reservations several days in advance to avoid the rush.

⑥ Spago Beverly Hills

A favorite with the rich and famous *(see p119)* and a great place to sample California cuisine *(see p54)*. The menu pairs supreme cuts of meat or fish with seasonal side dishes such as chanterelle mushrooms. The lox pizza is always popular. Early reservations essential.

⑦ Valentino

Since 1972, Piero Selvaggio has delighted diners with his charm. The restaurant offers classic Italian cuisine, updated for modern tastes without becoming Americanized. His 150,000 – plus cellar containing handpicked Italian wines is outstanding. So are the ingredients, many of them imported from Italy. Insiders ignore the menu and try the "extravaganza," a series of delicious treats.

Wine cellar private room, Valentino

Alfresco dining, Michael's

⑧ Michael's

A pioneer of California cuisine, Michael's serves Oscar-worthy cuisine in a luscious garden setting, making it one of the best alfresco dining spots in all LA. The food delights both the eye and palate. The decor harks back to its 1979 opening, but a new chef has brought contemporary tastes and ingredients to the menu.

⑨ Mélisse

Consistently ranked as the top food spot in LA, Josiah Citrin's two-Michelin-starred Mélisse uses fresh local ingredients to create classic French cuisine with a modern twist. Seasonal white truffle and game menus also feature. A gorgeous dining room and expertly trained staff add to a dining experience that borders on perfection, making this a top choice for memorable dinners.

⑩ Maude

You must reserve online over a month in advance to dine at Australian celebrity chef Curtis Stone's unassuming restaurant. Named after Stone's paternal grandmother, Maud has only 24 seats, an intimate and cozy atmosphere, and an incredibly friendly service. It is set up like a Chef's table where a different ingredient is featured every three months – pistachios, black truffles, or pomegranates, are a few examples – and a ten-course meal is derived from there. Each tasting menu also focuses on one of four of the world's top wine regions.

Top10 Shopping Streets

1 Third Street Promenade

A carnival atmosphere reigns on this popular pedestrian-only strip (see p121), especially during the summer months. Upscale chains such as Club Monaco and Anthropologie dominate, with a few bookstores and old-timers including the Puzzle Zoo toy store thrown in.

2 Montana Avenue

MAP B3 ■ Between 7th & 17th Sts, Santa Monica

You're likely to bump into celebrities in the upscale boutiques on Montana Avenue. It's fun peeking at the clothes, home furnishings, beauty products, and exercise gear favored by fashionistas.

3 Old Town Pasadena

Once an ancient crumbling historic district, Old Town Pasadena (see p93) was given a makeover in the 1990s. Today, Colorado Boulevard and its side streets offer pleasant shopping in mostly mid-priced chains and specialty stores.

4 Rodeo Drive

A stroll along this fabled Los Angeles shopping street (see p115) is a must. All the big names in haute couture have staked out their turf on Rodeo (see p118), including Ralph Lauren, Armani, Balenciaga, Valentino, Dolce & Gabbana, Chanel, and Versace. For better prices, walk just two blocks east to Beverly Drive.

Shopping on Robertson Boulevard

5 Robertson Boulevard

MAP L5 ■ Between 3rd St & Beverly Blvd

Price tags are steep at the boutiques on this ultracool two-block stretch, but you may be browsing next to celebrities such as Cameron Diaz or Jennifer Aniston. Part of the mix are cutting-edge LA designers.

6 Melrose Avenue

Tattooed 20-somethings buy vintage clothing, clubwear, and jewelry in stores between La Brea Boulevard and Fairfax Avenue (see p112). West of Fairfax is a designer enclave and the Pacific Design Center (see p109) is more about trendy home furnishings

The upmarket Rodeo Drive

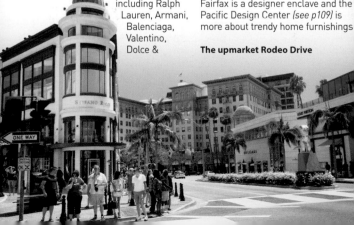

7 Main Street, Santa Monica

A laid-back yet sophisticated string of one-of-a-kind boutiques (with the odd chain store thrown in), Main Street *(see p125)* makes for a fun shopping experience with plenty of cafés for people-watching. On Sundays, catch the farmers' market.

8 Abbot Kinney Boulevard

MAP B5 ▪ Between Venice Blvd & Main St

The pint-sized stores here teem with character, not to mention characters. This is Venice, after all: laid-back, hip, and plenty artistic. Fans of 1950s furniture, New Agers in search of aura-enhancing elixirs, and gift shoppers will find all that they want.

Quirky shop, Abbot Kinney Boulevard

9 Santee Alley

MAP T6 ▪ Between Olympic Blvd & 12th St, Downtown

Bargain hunters will love this pedestrian-only lane, the busiest in the Fashion District and the center of LA's garment industry. In a setting reminiscent of an old bazaar, vendors hawk cut-rate clothing, accessories, and luggage. Alas, fakes are not uncommon, so beware.

10 West Third Street

MAP M5 ▪ Between La Cienega Blvd & Fairfax Ave, W Hollywood

Between the Beverly Center and the Original Farmers Market, this shopping strip is a mile-long and is one of the hippest in LA. The bounty ranges from gift stores such as New Stone Age to local LA-made fashions at Maison Nathalie Boutique.

TOP 10 SHOPPING MALLS

Shops at Santa Monica Place

1 Santa Monica Place
MAP B3 ▪ 310-394-5451
Frank Gehry-designed mall with great food courts.

2 Beverly Center
MAP L5 ▪ 310-854-0070
Upscale retail assortment within a fortress-like facade.

3 The Grove at Farmers Market
323-900-8000
Outdoor mall with mock streetscape and fountains *(see p107)*.

4 Glendale Galleria
MAP D1 ▪ 818-240-9481
Dedicated mall-crawlers will love the 250 mostly mid-priced stores.

5 Southcoast Plaza
MAP G4 ▪ 1-800-782-8888
Over 250 boutiques have made this mall one of the largest in the US – an international shopping destination.

6 Westfield Century City
MAP C2 ▪ 310-553-5300
Elegant shopping area with boutiques and valet parking.

7 The Paseo
MAP E1 ▪ 626-795-8891
Trendy Pasadena "urban village" with 50 stores, a movie theater, new Hyatt hotel and condos.

8 Hollywood & Highland
MAP P2 ▪ 323-467-6412
Choose between 70 stores and 25 restaurants beneath the Hollywood Sign at this outdoor mall in Tinseltown.

9 Westfield Fashion Square
MAP C1 ▪ 818-783-0550
Indoor mall that prides itself on outstanding service.

10 7th+Fig
MAP T5 ▪ 213-955-7150
Fun architecture, great food, and a colorful farmers' market on Thursdays.

TOP10 Los Angeles for Free

The famous Hollywood Sign in Hollywood Hills

1 Hike to the Hollywood Sign
www.hollywoodsign.org

Protected by a fence and security cameras, the famous 45-ft- (14-m-) tall aluminum letters cannot be reached, but you can get pretty close. Three trails wind upwards through native chaparral, home to abundant wildlife – chickadees and hawks, and occasional deer. Trails are graded easy to difficult, and vary in distance from 3–6.5 miles (5–10.5 km).

2 Downtown Art Walk
Walks noon–10pm, second Thu each month ■ www.downtown artwalk.org

Galleries and art exhibitions on Spring and Main between 2nd and 9th streets host an open house for the community with live music, talks and activities.

3 Griffith Observatory
Visiting the grounds and iconic Art Deco-style observatory (see pp34–5) are free to the public. City views are spectacular. Stargaze through the Zeiss telescope on a clear night or wonder at a

The iconic Griffith Observatory

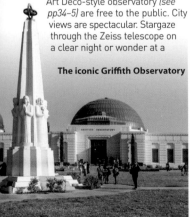

Foucault pendulum. Free public star parties are held monthly. There is no charge for parking.

4 Be in the Audience of a TV Show
www.tvtickets.com ■ www. on-camera-audiences.com

Free tickets to your favorite comedy, game, and talk shows are usually distributed on a first-come, first-served basis. Tickets to the more popular shows go fast, so it is advised to reserve in advance. If you are wandering around the Farmers Market or Grove shopping center, you may be approached to fill a seat at the nearby CBS Studio.

Aquarium, California Science Center

5 California Science Center

Free permanent exhibitions feature lots of hands-on activities. Examine an astronaut's suit; learn how bodily organs work together, and explore an underwater kelp forest and polar research station. This (see p86) is a great place for kids of all ages.

6 The Getty Center
This (see pp16–19) is one of LA's great community draws, offering fantastic city-wide views, art exhibitions, gardens, tours, and lectures. Many live musical performances are free too. You only pay for parking, but LA Metro buses stop right at the entrance.

Exhibit at the Page Museum

7 La Brea Tar Pits
5801 Wilshire Blvd ▪ 323-857-6300 ▪ www.tarpits.org

You can wander around the tar pits and the life-size prehistoric animal models, and contemplate the 40,000 years of hot bubbling asphalt without charge, but paid admission is required for the adjacent Page Museum and its impressive fossil collection.

8 Hollywood Bowl Free Rehearsals

During the summer on Tuesday, Thursday, and some Friday mornings from 9am to noon, you can sit in the historic bowl *(see p100)* and watch rehearsals. The outdoor setting is gorgeous, so bring a picnic lunch. The adjacent Hollywood Bowl Museum is also free.

9 Visit Gravesites of the Stars
www.seeing-stars.com/buried

The final resting places of famous movie stars are located across the LA area. Hollywood Forever hands out a map to help you find your favorite celebrity. All are open to the public.

10 Free Music Concerts at LACMA

LACMA *(see pp20–23)* sponsors free one-hour concerts every weekend. From April to November, you'll hear jazz on Friday nights and classical on Sundays. Concerts start at 5 or 6pm. From June to August, on Saturday evenings, it's Latin music. Venues are either the BP Grand Entrance or the Bing Theatre.

TOP 10 BUDGET TIPS

1 Free Museum Days
Many museums that are free one day a week or once a month.

2 Theater Tickets
www.theatreinla.com
Get half price theater tickets for selected plays through Theatre in LA.

3 Go Los Angeles Card
www.smartdestinations.com
A 1- to 7-day pass to nearly 30 attractions, museums, and tours.

4 Shop at Farmers' Markets
Put together a picnic of reasonably priced fresh, local food from outdoor markets located throughout LA.

5 Happy Hour
On late weekday afternoons, many restaurants offer discounted menu items in the bar area.

6 Senior discounts
Senior citizens qualify for substantial discounts on transportation, museum admissions, movies, and Hollywood Bowl concerts.

7 Get Rid of the Rental Car at Disneyland
If staying multiple days, you don't need a car. Anaheim hotels run free or low-cost shuttles to Disneyland.

8 Save on Parking
Selected lots at Metro Rail and Metrolink stations have free parking for transit users.

9 Disney Tickets
Credit unions, teacher unions, and the Auto Club sometimes offer slightly discounted tickets. Never buy a partly used pass from anybody.

10 Save on Gas
GasBuddy (www.gasbuddy.com) has up-to-date prices for all local gas stations.

ARCO gas station

TOP 10 Drives and Day Trips

1 Mulholland Drive
MAP C1

Named after William Mulholland, the architect of the Los Angeles aqueduct, this quintessential LA road winds for about 25 miles (40 km) along a Santa Monica Mountains ridge from Hollywood to the western San Fernando Valley. On clear days, the panoramic views over Los Angeles county are truly stunning.

2 Mission San Gabriel Arcangel
MAP E2 ▪ 428 S Mission Dr, San Gabriel ▪ 626-457-3035 ▪ Open 9am–4:30pm daily ▪ Adm

Heavy flooding forced the fourth of the California missions to move here five years after it was founded in 1771. Though struck twice by earthquakes, it prospered with the help of Indian converts, many of whom are buried here. The grounds are peppered with fountains and fireplaces. A small museum has other exhibits.

Mission San Fernando Rey de España

4 Mission San Fernando Rey de España
15151 San Fernando Mission Blvd, Mission Hills ▪ 818-361-0186 ▪ Open 9am–4:30pm daily ▪ Adm

The 17th of the 21 missions founded by Franciscans in California, San Fernando was established in 1797 to supply food for El Pueblo de Los Angeles. The mission church is an exact replica of the original, destroyed in the 1971 Sylmar earthquake. The adjacent *convento* (living quarters) is the state's largest surviving adobe structure.

Knott's Berry Farm entrance

3 Knott's Berry Farm
8039 Beach Blvd, Buena Park ▪ 714-220-5200 ▪ Check website for opening hours ▪ www.knotts.com

The first theme park in the US, Old West-themed Knott's Berry Farm is known for its gut-wrenching roller coasters. Teens love the Xcelerator and the Supreme Scream, while Camp Snoopy charms younger children. Five themed areas offer entertainment for all ages.

5 Six Flags Magic Mountain
26101 Magic Mountain Parkway, Valencia ▪ 661-255-4104 ▪ Open late Mar–early Sep: 12:30–6pm daily; rest of the year: weekends & hols ▪ Adm ▪ www.sixflags.com

The Holy Grail for roller-coaster junkies, Six Flags has more ways to catapult, spin, loop, spiral, and twist than you or your stomach can imagine. Favorite white-knuckle rides include X, the world's first four-dimensional coaster, and Superman: The Escape, which has you free-falling for 6.5 seconds.

6 Santa Barbara and Wine Country

On Hwy 101, about 90 miles (145 km) north of LA

This town, with its Spanish-style architecture and villa-studded hillsides, is quite charming. Apart from the mission building and historical adobes, it is also a must visit for wine connoisseurs. Head for the tasting rooms of the wine country around Santa Ynez, a 45-minute drive away.

7 Queen Mary

MAP E4 ■ 1126 Queen Hwy, Long Beach ■ 800-437-2934 ■ Open 10am–6pm ■ Adm ■ www.queenmary.com

The *Queen Mary* has whisked as many as 15,000 soldiers per trip from the USA to Europe during World War II. Retired in 1964, she became a tourist attraction three years later. Much of the Queen Mary, which also contains a hotel, can be explored on self-guided tours.

8 Ventura and Channel Islands National Park

On Hwy 101, about 65 miles (105 km) north of LA

Ventura's Main Street is a fun place to browse antiques and second-hand stores. A look inside the Mission San Buenaventura is worthwhile. The town is the gateway to the Channel Islands National Park. Excursions to the islands leave from Ventura Harbor year-round.

9 Nixon Presidential Library and Museum

18001 Yorba Linda Blvd, Yorba Linda ■ 714-993-3393 ■ Open 10am–5pm daily (from 11am Sun) ■ Adm ■ www.nixonlibrary.gov

This memorial to the 37th US president (1913–94) includes a museum, gardens, and the restored 1910 farmhouse where he was born. Exhibits focus on Nixon's achievements, but also include a gallery about Watergate. A re-creation of the Lincoln Sitting Room is a highlight.

10 Ronald Reagan Presidential Library and Museum

40 Presidential Dr, Simi Valley ■ 800-410-8354 ■ Open 10am–5pm daily ■ Adm ■ www.reaganlibrary.net

A chunk of the Berlin Wall and a re-created Oval Office are the highlights of this museum devoted to the 40th US president (1911–2004). Exhibits trace Reagan's life from his childhood, through his Hollywood career to his political ascent.

Ventura and Channel Islands National Park

Los Angeles
Area by Area

The Griffith Observatory overlooking
Downtown Los Angeles

Downtown	**76**
Around Downtown	**84**
Pasadena	**90**
Hollywood	**98**
West Hollywood and Midtown	**106**
Beverly Hills, Westwood, and Bel-Air	**114**
Santa Monica Bay	**120**
Coastal Orange County	**128**

ᴛᴏᴘ10 Downtown

Downtown LA is a microcosm of the city's past, present, and future. El Pueblo commemorates the city's Spanish origins, while Chinatown and Little Tokyo are vibrant communities. The city's financial center, along Flower and Figueroa streets, sits in sharp contrast to the early 20th-century architecture around Pershing Square. Cultural sites include the renowned Museum of Contemporary Art, the Walt Disney Concert Hall, and the galleries of the Arts District. The Fashion and Jewelry districts also add their own flair, and Downtown is dominated by L.A. Live, a vast sports and entertainment district.

Olvera Street souvenir

DOWNTOWN

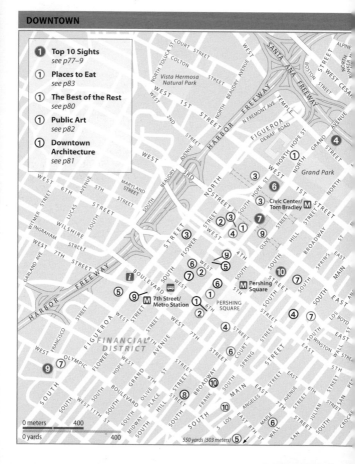

1 **Top 10 Sights**
see p77–9

1 **Places to Eat**
see p83

1 **The Best of the Rest**
see p80

1 **Public Art**
see p82

1 **Downtown Architecture**
see p81

1 El Pueblo de Los Angeles

This historic district (see pp24–5) near LA's 1781 founding site comprises buildings dating back to the early 19th century, when the city was just an outpost under Mexican rule. Its main artery, Olvera Street, has been restored to a lively lane lined with Mexican trinket shops and restaurants.

2 Union Station
MAP X4 ■ 800 N Alameda St

Built in 1939 during the golden age of railroad travel, Union Station blends traditional Spanish Mission elements with Modernist Art Deco

One of Union Station's grand halls

touches. Its lofty main waiting room is graced with a coffered wooden ceiling, highly polished marble floors, and tall arched windows. Union Station has been featured In several movies, *The Hustler* (1961) and *Bugsy* (1991) among others.

3 City Hall
MAP W4 ■ 200 N Spring St ■ Open 8am–5pm Mon–Fri ■ Guided tours: 10am–noon

This was LA's tallest building for over four decades, with the central tower of this 1928 complex three times higher than the height limit at that time. Renovations have made it possible for the public to admire its marble-columned rotunda once again. City Hall has been immortalized on celluloid countless times, most famously as the headquarters of the *Daily Planet* in the *Superman* TV series. It was also attacked by Martians in *The War of the Worlds* (1953).

Los Angeles City Hall

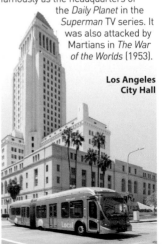

4 Cathedral of Our Lady of the Angels

MAP V3 ▪ 555 W Temple St ▪ 213-680-5200 ▪ Open 6:30am–6pm Mon–Fri, 9am–6pm Sat, 7am–6pm Sun ▪ Free tours: 1pm Mon–Fri ▪ www.olacathedral.org

LA's strikingly modern Roman Catholic cathedral looms above the Hollywood Freeway. Enter through giant bronze doors cast by LA sculptor Robert Graham and guarded by a statue of Our Lady of the Angels. The interior of the cathedral is bathed in a soft light that streams in through the alabaster windows.

5 Little Tokyo

MAP W5 ▪ Bounded by 1st & 4th, Alameda, & Los Angeles Sts

The Japanese have been a presence in LA since the 1880s, but redevelopment in the 1960s replaced most of Little Tokyo with bland modern architecture. The few surviving buildings on East First Street are now a National Historic Landmark. Stop at the Japanese American National Museum, and check out the MOCA Geffen Contemporary (see p80).

6 Walt Disney Concert Hall

MAP V4 ▪ 111 S Grand Ave ▪ 323-850-2000 ▪ www.laphil.com

A spectacular addition to Downtown's landscape is the home of the Los Angeles Philharmonic Orchestra. Frank Gehry conceived the dramatic auditorium (see p64), rather like the sculptural interpretation of a ship at sea. The exterior "sails" are clad in stainless-steel panels, while the hall itself (see p48) boasts a curved wooden ceiling with superb acoustics.

Art exhibit at MOCA

7 Museum of Contemporary Art (MOCA)

MAP U4 ▪ 250 S Grand Ave ▪ 213-626-6222 ▪ Open 11am–5pm Sat & Sun, 11am–8pm Thu, 11am–6pm Mon, Wed & Fri ▪ Adm (free after 5pm on Thu) ▪ www.moca.org

An early player in Downtown's cultural renaissance, MOCA collects and displays art in all media from 1940 to the present, in a building designed by famous Japanese architect Arata Isozaki. Works by Jackson Pollock, Andy Warhol, and Roy Lichtenstein form part of its permanent collection.

8 Chinatown

MAP W2 ▪ Along Broadway Hill north of Cesar Chavez Blvd

The Chinese first settled in LA after the Gold Rush, but were forced by the construction of Union Station to relocate a few blocks north to an area that is today known as "New Chinatown." The cultural hub of over 200,000 Chinese Americans, this exotic district sells everything from pickled ginger to lucky bamboo.

Colorful buildings of Chinatown

CHUNG KING ROAD GALLERIES

This quiet, lantern-festooned lane in western Chinatown is the hotbed of LA's art scene. Artists' studios and several galleries have opened in between the traditional Chinese antique and furniture stores in the area. Follow a browsing session with a quiet drink at the Hop Louie restaurant.

⑨ L.A. Live Sports and Entertainment District

MAP S6

A 4,000,000-sq-ft (371,600-sq-m) development, adjoining the Staples Center and the Los Angeles Convention Center, houses LA's premier sports and entertainment district. Venues include the Microsoft Theater, with state of the-art acoustics and seating for 7,200 people, and The Novo by Microsoft, a live music venue. At the heart of the center is Microsoft Square.

Fresh produce, Grand Central Market

⑩ Grand Central Market

MAP V5 ■ 317 S Broadway ■ 213-624-2378 ■ Open 9am–6pm daily ■ www.grandcentralsquare.com

Angelenos have perused the produce aisles of this exotic and lively market since 1917. Today, visitors stock up on everything from fruits and vegetables to fresh fish and meat, and spices and herbs to cakes and bread, all available at bargain prices. Many of the eateries here also have long traditions, such as Roast-to-Go, where the Penilla family has served tacos and burritos since the 1950s. The architect Frank Lloyd Wright once had an office upstairs.

A DAY IN DOWNTOWN

▶ MORNING

Begin your day with the historic **El Pueblo** (see p77), which will take you back to the city's vibrant Mexican and Spanish past. Browse colorful **Olvera Street** (see p24) for authentic crafts and food, and then cross Alameda Street for a close-up of the grand **Union Station** (see p77).

Next, go west along Cesar E. Chavez Avenue, before turning right on Broadway for a stroll through exotic **Chinatown** and a superb lunch at the **Philippe's the Original** (see p83).

AFTERNOON

Ride the DASH bus "B" from Broadway to Temple Street, dominated by the **Cathedral of Our Lady of the Angels**. After admiring Rafael Moneo's Modernist masterpiece, head south along Grand Avenue, past the **Music Center** (see p64) and the **Walt Disney Concert Hall** to check out the latest exhibits at the **MOCA**.

Stroll down **Bunker Hill Steps** (see p81), stopping to gaze at Source Figure, Robert Graham's exquisite sculpture and the **Central Library** (see p80). Walk to Pershing Square, lorded over by the baronial **Millennium Biltmore Hotel** (see p81), a nice place for tea or coffee. Leave in time to make it to the Victorian **Bradbury Building** (see p49) before 5pm. Browse for treasures in the bountiful aisles of the **Grand Central Market**.

See map on pp76–7 ←

The Best of the Rest

1 Wells Fargo History Museum

MAP U4 ■ 333 S Grand Ave ■ Open 9am–5pm Mon–Fri

A Wild West museum housing an original stagecoach and a gold nugget from the Gold Rush.

2 Central Library

MAP U5 ■ 630 W 5th St ■ 213-228-7000 ■ Open 10am–8pm Mon–Thu, 9:30am–5:30pm Fri–Sat, 1–5pm Sun

LA's main library consists of the original 1926 building, a Beaux-Arts design by Bertram Goodhue, and an art-filled atrium added in 1993.

Reading room, Central Library

3 The Broad

MAP V4 ■ 221 S Grand Ave ■ 213-232-6200 ■ Opening times vary, check website ■ www.the broad.org

A superb contemporary art collection housed in a striking building. Yayoi Kusama's dazzling *Infinity Mirrored Room* is especially popular.

4 Jewelry District

MAP U5 ■ Hill St just off Pershing Square

Precious gems, watches, and fine jewels are sold in shops in what has long been the center of Los Angeles's jewelry industry.

5 Fashion District

MAP U6 ■ Bounded by Broadway, San Pedro St, 7th St, & 16th St

The 56-block district *(see p69)* is the heart of LA's clothing industry and heaven on earth for bargain hunters.

6 Flower Market

MAP V6 ■ 766 Wall St ■ 213-627-3696 ■ Opening times vary ■ Adm ■ www.originallaflower market.com

This 1913 cut-flower market, the largest in the country, has it all from roses to orchids.

7 The Grammy Museum

MAP S6 ■ 800 W Olympic Blvd ■ 213-765-6800 ■ Open 10:30am–6:30pm Sun–Thu, 10am–8pm Fri & Sat ■ www.grammymuseum.org

You can record and perform a song at this interactive museum dedicated to the music industry.

8 Japanese American National Museum

MAP W5 ■ 100 N Central Ave ■ 213-625-0414 ■ Open 11am–5pm Tue, Wed, Fri–Sun, noon–8pm Thu ■ Adm ■ www.janm.org

Housed in a Buddhist temple, this museum chronicles the history of Japanese Americans.

9 MOCA Geffen Contemporary

MAP W5 ■ 152 N Central Ave ■ 213-626-6222 ■ Open 11am–6pm Wed & Fri, 11am–8pm Thu, 11am–5pm Sat & Sun ■ Adm (except 5–8pm Thu) ■ www.moca.org

This huge former police garage hosts traveling shows and exhibits.

10 Downtown Arts District

MAP U4 ■ Bounded by 1st & 7th Sts, Alameda Ave, & the Los Angeles River

As artists have moved into studios here, trendy galleries, shops, and restaurants have also opened.

Downtown Architecture

1 Oviatt Building
MAP U5 ▪ 617 S Olive St

This 1927 Art Deco gem *(see p83)* has French fixtures and a forecourt decorated with Lalique glass. It houses the popular Cicada restaurant.

2 Coca-Cola Bottling Plant
MAP E3 ▪ 1334 S Central Ave
▪ Not open to the public

A Streamline Moderne building, located in an industrial area, this resembles an ocean liner, complete with porthole windows. Two giant Coke bottles guard the corners.

3 Westin Bonaventure Hotel & Suites
MAP U4 ▪ 404 S Figueroa St
▪ 213-624-1000

The five mirror-glass cylinders of LA's biggest hotel *(see p148)* look like a space ship ready for take-off.

4 Old Bank District
MAP V5 ▪ On 4th St between Main & Spring Sts

This trio of statuesque buildings, built between 1904 and 1910, has been converted into residential lofts.

5 US Bank Tower
MAP U5 ▪ 633 W 5th St

Standing at 1,017 ft (310 m), this building was erected only after developers were forced to purchase the air rights from neighboring Central Library in order to exceed official height limits.

US Bank Tower skyscraper

Interior of Millennium Biltmore Hotel

6 Millennium Biltmore Hotel
MAP U5 ▪ 506 S Grand Ave
▪ 213-624-1011

A range of architectural styles, from Renaissance to Neo-Classical, adorn this 1923 Beaux-Arts hotel.

7 Bunker Hill Steps
MAP U4

Cascading from Hope Street to Fifth Street, these steps *(see p82)* have many features, including a sculpture of a female nude by Robert Graham.

8 Eastern Columbia Building
MAP U6 ▪ 849 Broadway

A bright turquoise terracotta mantle covers this former 1930s furniture and clothing store.

9 Fine Arts Building
MAP T5 ▪ 811 W 7th St Lobby
▪ Open during office hours

Behind the richly detailed façade of this 1927 building awaits a galleried lobby in Spanish Renaissance style.

10 Broadway Historic Theater District
MAP U6 ▪ Along Broadway between 3rd & 9th Sts

During the silent-film era, Broadway was the most popular movie district. The movie palaces here are architectural marvels.

See map on pp76–7 ←

Public Art

1 Peace on Earth
MAP V4 ▪ Music Center Plaza, 135 N Grand Ave
Created at the height of the Vietnam War in 1969, Jacques Lipchitz's bronze Madonna has the dove, a symbol of peace, on top, and lambs, representing humanity, at the base.

2 Four Arches
MAP U4 ▪ 333 S Hope St
Alexander Calder is best known for his suspended mobiles, but this looming 1975 steel work painted in glowing fiery orange-red is a "stabile," an abstract stationary sculpture.

3 Wells Fargo Court
MAP U4 ▪ Wells Fargo Center, 333 S Grand Ave
The ground floor of this office complex is a treasure trove of public art with nudes by Robert Graham, Joan Miró's childlike *La Caresse d'un Oiseau*, and Jean Dubuffet's cartoonish *Le Dandy*.

Peace on Earth

5 Corporate Head
MAP T5 ▪ 725 S Figueroa St
An evocative sculpture (1990) by Terry Allen and Philip Levine, this condemns the greed and erosion of moral responsibility in today's corporate America.

6 Spine
MAP U4 ▪ Maguire Gardens, northern side of Central Library, Flower, & 5th Sts
Jud Fine's 1993 installation is a visual allegory of a book – the well symbolizes the title page, the steps the pages, and the pools the plot flow.

7 Biddy Mason: A Passage of Time
MAP V5 ▪ 333 S Spring St, near 3rd St
This memorial by Betye Saar and Sheila de Bretteville commemorates the story of former slave, Biddy Mason (1818–91), who established the city's first black church.

8 Astronaut Ellison S. Onizuka Memorial
MAP W5 ▪ Onizuka St, Little Tokyo
A 1/10th scale model of the *Challenger*, this 1990 memorial by Isao Hirai honors the first Japanese-American astronaut.

9 Source Figure
MAP U4 ▪ Hope St, near 4th St
Overlooking the Bunker Hill Steps (see p81) stands this bronze African-American female nude. Designed by Robert Graham in 1992, she represents the source of the water cascading down the stairs.

10 Traveler
MAP X4 ▪ Union Station
Terry Schoonhoven's 1993 ceramic mural (see p25) depicts California travelers from the days of the Spanish explorations, and LA landmarks such as Pico House.

Molecule Man by Jonathan Borofsky

4 Molecule Man
MAP W4 ▪ 255 E Temple St
This monumental sculpture by Jonathan Borofsky shows four embracing figures, symbolizing the commonality between people based on their shared molecular structure.

Places to Eat

PRICE CATEGORIES
Price categories include a three-course meal for one, a glass of house wine, and all unavoidable extra charges including tax.

$ under $25 $$ $25–$50 $$$ $50–$80
$$$$ over $80

1 Water Grill
MAP U5 ▪ 544 S Grand Ave
▪ 213-891-0900 ▪ $$$

Fish and seafood fanciers from all over flock to this clubby shrine, which uses only impeccably fresh ingredients. Desserts are superb.

2 Cicada
MAP U5 ▪ 617 S Olive St
▪ 213-488-9488 ▪ $$$

The sumptuous Art Deco dining room in the historic Oviatt Building almost overshadows the food. The menu features north Italian classics.

3 Patina
MAP U4 ▪ Walt Disney Concert Hall, 141 S Grand Ave ▪ 213-972-3331
▪ $$$

Expect the latest innovations in French-Californian cuisine and be prepared to reserve far in advance.

4 Nick & Stef's Steakhouse
MAP U4 ▪ 330 S Hope St, Wells Fargo Center ▪ 213-680-0330 ▪ $$$

Loosen your belt for the juiciest steaks ever. Preview your cut in the glass-encased aging chamber.

5 Philippe's the Original
MAP X3 ▪ 1001 N Alameda St
▪ 213-628-3781 ▪ $

Philippe's has served its famous French-dipped sandwiches since 1908. Seating is at long communal tables. Limited vegetarian options.

6 Clifton's Cafeteria
MAP U5 ▪ 648 S Broadway
▪ 213-627-1673 ▪ $

LA institution with rustic woodland decor and plenty of taxidermy. Upstairs has themed cocktail bars.

7 Bäco Mercat
MAP V5 ▪ 408 S Main St
▪ 213-687-8808 ▪ $$

Chef Josef Centeno masters the flavors of the Mediterranean and Spain at his trendy diner. Choose the signature "bäco" flatbread sandwich.

Stylish dining room at Bäco Mercat

8 Yang Chow
MAP W2 ▪ 819 N Broadway, Chinatown ▪ 213-625-0811 ▪ $

In this reliable Chinese eatery, a plate of the hallmark "slippery shrimp" graces almost every table. The *moo-shu* pork is also a good bet.

9 Noe
MAP X4 ▪ 251 S Olive St
▪ 213-356-4100 ▪ $$$$

A romantic place for post-theater dining, Noe offers fresh seafood, meats, and poultry prepared in an American-Japanese fusion style.

10 Casa La Doña
MAP U6 ▪ 800 S Main St
▪ 213-627-7441 ▪ Open daily, breakfast only Fri–Sun ▪ $

A salsa bar with truly authentic regional dishes from Mexico, home-made tortillas, tamales, and spot-on service. Try the fresh blue-gill fish.

See map on pp76–7

🔟 Around Downtown

It has been said that LA is not really a city, but a collection of 88 independent towns that overlap. Nowhere is this truer than within the 5-mile (8-km) radius of Downtown. West of here, Koreatown is home to the largest Korean population in the US, while east LA has the largest group of Latinos living outside Latin America. In the Latino-Byzantine quarter, surrounding St. Sophia Cathedral, Latinos and Greeks predominate. Northeast is Dodger Stadium, a world-famous landmark, while south of the center is Exposition Park with its museums and sports venues.

Hale House, Heritage Square Museum

① Heritage Square Museum

MAP E2 ■ 3800 Homer St, Highland Park ■ 323-225-2700 ■ Open 11:30am–4:30pm Fri–Sun (Oct–Mar: hours may vary, call for details) ■ Adm ■ www.heritagesquare.org

Apart from those on Carroll Avenue, most Victorian homes in LA were demolished. A few, however, were moved by helicopter to form the Heritage Square Museum. Eight vintage beauties cluster here, with Hale House, the most outstanding.

AROUND DOWNTOWN

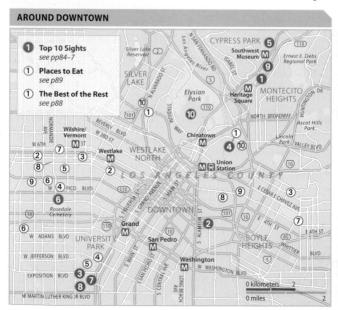

① Top 10 Sights
see pp84–7

① Places to Eat
see p89

① The Best of the Rest
see p88

Entrance to the San Antonio Winery, the last of its kind in Los Angeles

2 Institute of Contemporary Art LA

MAP V6 ■ 1717 E 17th St ■ 213-928-0833 ■ Open 11am–7pm Wed–Fri, 11am–6pm Sat–Sun ■ www.the icala.org

Founded in 1984 as the Santa Monica Museum of Art, this museum opened at its new location in 2017 and has played a crucial role in the revitalization of downtown. Exhibitions feature contemporary artists from around the world and reflect the cultural diversity and energy of the city. The facility also offers an open-air courtyard and café.

3 Natural History Museum

MAP D3 ■ 900 Exposition Blvd, Exposition Park ■ 213-763-3466 ■ Open 9:30am–5pm daily ■ Adm (free for under 5s) ■ www.nhm.org

Spend a day exploring this engaging museum where the dinosaurs always draw huge crowds, as does the Age of Mammals exhibit with the Simi Valley mastodon, and the 14.5-ft (4-m) long megamouth, the rarest shark in the world. The Gem and Mineral Hall contains a huge gold exhibit and a walk-through gem vault. Cultural exhibits explain and highlight the traditions of Native and Latin American civilizations. Children love the hands-on activities in the Discovery Center and the Insect Zoo.

4 San Antonio Winery

MAP E2 ■ 737 Lamar St, Lincoln Heights ■ 323-223-1401 ■ Tasting room: open 9am–7pm Sun–Thu, 9am–8pm Fri & Sat ■ www.sanantoniowinery.com

LA's only surviving winery (see p89) is tucked away in the industrial area north of the Los Angeles River, an area once blanketed with vineyards. When founder Santo Cambianica arrived in 1917, he faced competition from over 100 wineries. Prohibition put most out of business, but Santo survived making sacramental wine. Taste the wines and try the restaurant – a popular lunch spot.

Southwest Museum of the American Indian

5 Southwest Museum of the American Indian

MAP E2 ■ 234 Museum Dr, Highland Park ■ 323-221-2164 ■ Open 10am–4pm Sat (call for details) ■ www.theautry.org

The oldest museum in Los Angeles was the brainchild of Charles Lummis, whose collection of Native American artifacts formed the basis of its holdings. It has one of the nation's largest collections of Native art and artifacts. Galleries provide a survey of the traditions of Native cultures from California, the Great Plains, the Southwest, and the Pacific Northwest. Restoration work is ongoing; call ahead for details.

The impressive altar and religious iconography at St. Sophia Cathedral

6 St. Sophia Cathedral
MAP D2 ■ 1324 S Normandie Ave, Koreatown ■ 323-737-2424 ■ Open 10am–4pm Tue–Fri, 10am–2pm Sat , 12:30–2pm Sun ■ www.stsophia.org

One of LA's surprises, this central church of Southern California's Greek Orthodox community is an opulent hall of worship. The eye is drawn to the icon-studded, golden altar of the Virgin Mary, while Jesus, surrounded by saints, looks down at the congregation from the 90-ft (27-m) high dome.

California African American Museum

7 California African American Museum
MAP D2 ■ 600 State Dr, Exposition Park ■ 213-744-7432 ■ Open 10am–5pm Tue–Sat, 11am–5pm Sun ■ Parking $10 ■ www.caamuseum.org

This museum celebrates the art, history, and culture of African Americans, especially in relation to California and the western US. The main exhibit traces the journey from Africa to slavery throughout America to final freedom on the West Coast. Exhibits here highlight the contributions made by African-American artists to American culture.

8 California Science Center
MAP D2 ■ 700 State Drive, Exposition Park ■ 323-724-3623 ■ Open 10am–5pm daily ■ Parking $10 ■ www.californiasciencecenter.org

Filled with clever and engaging interactive exhibits, this highly entertaining science and technology museum (see p58) has three themed galleries. The World of Life exhibit explains the processes living organisms undergo, Creative World focuses on the ability of humans to adapt to their environment through technology, and the Air and Space Gallery explores the great beyond. But it's the Space Shuttle *Endeavour* that steals the show and attracts the crowds.

9 Charles F. Lummis Home and Garden
MAP E2 ■ 200 E Ave 43, Highland Park ■ 323-222-0546 ■ Open 10am–3pm Sat–Sun ■ Donation

Now the headquarters of the Historical Society of Southern California, this was once the home of the eccentric Charles Fletcher Lummis (1859–1928), who walked the entire 3,000 miles (4,830 km)

KOREATOWN

Parts of western Vermont Avenue around Wilshire Boulevard west of Downtown would not look out of place in Seoul. These are the main arteries of Koreatown, home to the largest Korean population in the US and a beehive of commercial activity. Learn more about the Korean community at the Korean Cultural Center at 5505 Wilshire Blvd.

from Ohio to LA in 1885. An outspoken California booster and preservationist, Lummis built his house with his own hands out of concrete and found materials, including boulders and railroad rails. The house is also known as El Alisal, Spanish for "sycamore," due to the giant sycamore by the building.

🔟 Dodger Stadium

MAP W1 ▪ 1000 Elysian Park Ave ▪ 323-224-1448 ▪ Tours (on non-game days by appointment only), tickets required ▪ www.dodgers.mlb.com/la/ballpark

For many, spring wouldn't be the same without baseball. The pilgrimage to Dodger Stadium to watch the "Boys in Blue" fight it out is an annual ritual for thousands of fans. Hunkered in the bleachers, munching on the famous Dodger Dogs, they watch their team (the LA Dodgers) in action. The stadium opened in 1962 and is often called one of US's most beautiful ballparks. It has hosted the World Series, many concerts, and even a papal mass.

Dodger Stadium on a match day

EXPLORING EXPOSITION PARK IN A DAY

▶ MORNING

Start at **Exposition Park** from Figueroa Street and make the **Natural History Museum** (see p85) the first stop of the day. Admire its lovely facade, before delving into the exhibits inside. A landmark bronze sculpture of a *Tyrannosaurus rex* battling a *Triceratops* stands to the north outside. Crossing the street takes you to the **University of Southern California** campus (see p88), where you can join a free guided tour offered hourly from 10am to 3pm. Have lunch on Exposition Boulevard or at the **Mercado La Paloma** (3655 S Grand Ave), a Latin-style community center with colorful crafts stalls and casual eating outlets.

AFTERNOON

Backtrack to Exposition Park and start the afternoon with a look at the **Los Angeles Memorial Coliseum** (3911 S Figueroa St), the main venue of the 1932 and 1984 Olympics. The two huge headless bronze figures outside the eastern entrance were designed by local sculptor Robert Graham. Just north of this spot is the **California Science Center**, with many interactive exhibits. Grab a cold drink from the cafeteria downstairs and head outside to the fragrant **Rose Garden** (see p52) to relax. If you still have the energy left, do check out the store at the **California African American Museum**. Otherwise, wind down the day with a 3-D adventure at the **IMAX Theater** (see p62) next to the Science Center.

See map on p84 ←

The Best of the Rest

1 Angelus Temple
MAP E1 ■ 1100 Glendale Blvd, Echo Park ■ Open only during special events

Founded by a popular preacher with a flair for theatrics, this 1923 domed building was once the headquarters of the Foursquare Gospel Church.

2 The Wiltern
MAP D2 ■ 3790 Wilshire Blvd, Koreatown

A live concert venue, encased by the 1931 Art Deco Pelissier Building.

3 Bullocks Wilshire Building
MAP D2 ■ 3050 Wilshire Blvd, Koreatown

One of the earliest Art Deco structures anywhere in the United States, this beautiful building is now home to the Southwestern University School of Law.

4 Shrine Auditorium
MAP D2 ■ 665 W Jefferson Blvd, Exposition Park area

This 1926 Moorish-style theater seats up to 6,700 and was once the largest in the US.

5 University of Southern California (USC)
MAP D2 ■ Bounded by Jefferson, Figueroa, Exposition Blvds & Vermont Ave, Exposition Park area ■ 213-740-2311 ■ www.usc.edu

Built in 1880, the oldest private university in Western US counts George Lucas among its alumni.

6 William Andrews Clark Memorial Library
MAP D2 ■ 2520 Cimarron St, W Adams district ■ 323-735-7605 ■ Tours by appointment

This 1926 building has a rare collection of English books only available to scholars, and an oak-paneled music room.

7 El Mercado
MAP E2 ■ 3425 E 1st St, E LA ■ 323-268-3451 ■ Open 10am–8pm Mon–Fri, 9am–9pm Sat & Sun

Stop for an authentic meal or browse colorful stalls at this Mexican-American indoor marketplace.

8 Self Help Graphics & Arts
MAP E2 ■ 1300 E First St, E LA ■ 323-881-6444 ■ Gallery hours: 9am–5pm Tue–Fri, 10am–4pm Sat

This nonprofit arts center works with the Latino community on printmaking, workshops, and exhibitions.

9 Mariachi Plaza
MAP E2 ■ Corner of Boyle Ave & 1st St, E LA

Mariachi musicians in black robes gather in this small park, waiting to be hired for the night's engagements.

10 Brewery Arts Complex
MAP E2 ■ 2100 N Main St, Lincoln Heights ■ 323-441-9593 ■ Gallery open Fri–Sun (by appointment only)

Art walks are organized twice yearly at this massive artists' colony.

University of Southern California

Places to Eat

1 Maddalena Restaurant
MAP E2 ■ 737 Lamar St, Lincoln Heights ■ 323-223-1401 ■ Lunch and early dinner (closes 7pm Sun–Thu & 8pm Sat) ■ Tours daily ■ $$

This slice of Italy, in what was once the cellars of the San Antonio Winery (see p85), is a popular lunch spot.

Maddalena Restaurant

2 Langer's Delicatessen
MAP E2 ■ 704 S Alvarado St ■ 213-483-8050 ■ Closed Sun ■ $

Award-winning Jewish deli serving LA's best pastrami sandwich.

3 El Tepeyac Café
MAP E2 ■ 812 N Evergreen Ave, E LA ■ 323-267-8668 ■ No credit cards ■ $

Long lines form outside LA's burrito "head-quarters" for the "Hollenbeck," stuffed with guacamole and pork.

Burritos, El Tepeyac

4 Papa Cristo's Taverna
MAP D2 ■ 2771 W Pico Blvd, Koreatown ■ 323-737-2970 ■ Closed Mon ■ $

Drop into this friendly, busy eatery next door to St. Sophia (see p86) for fat portions of great Greek food.

5 Soot Bull Jeep
MAP D2 ■ 3136 8th St, Koreatown ■ 213-387-3865 ■ $

Grill your own deliciously marinated meat at this authentic Korean spot.

PRICE CATEGORIES
Price categories include a three-course meal for one, a glass of house wine, and all unavoidable extra charges including tax.

$ under $25 $$ $25–$50 $$$ $50–$80
$$$$ over $80

---

6 Guelaguetza
MAP D2 ■ 3014 W Olympic Blvd, Koreatown ■ 213-427-0601 ■ $

This lively restaurant serving food from southern Mexico is famous for its *moles* – sauces made from spices, nuts, chilies, and chocolate.

7 HMS Bounty
MAP D2 ■ 3357 Wilshire Blvd ■ 213-385-7275 ■ $$

Popular historic local hangout with retro chic. Steaks, pub food, and cheap drinks are served up in nautical surroundings. Film shoots take place here once in a while.

8 Taylor's Steakhouse
MAP D2 ■ 3361 W 8th St, Koreatown ■ 213-382-8449 ■ $$

Send your cholesterol count through the roof at this venerable throwback to the 1950s, with faux leather booths and huge yummy steaks almost the size of baseball mitts.

9 El Cholo
MAP D2 ■ 1121 S Western Ave, Koreatown ■ 323-734-2773 ■ $

This festive Mexican eatery has been full of diners hungry for fajitas and burritos since 1923. Their margaritas pack a wicked punch.

10 Taix French Country Cuisine
MAP D2 ■ 1911 Sunset Blvd, Echo Park ■ 213-484-1265 ■ $$

This family-owned 1927 eatery serves good-value portions of French country classics, which include such dishes as delicious roast chicken with *bordelaise* sauce. Great soups.

See map on p84

🔟 Pasadena

Pasadena may be considered part of LA, but it is, in fact, distinctly apart. As the city's first suburb, it attracted a large share of the rich, who saw to it that a European flair enhanced the town. Fine mansions, such as the Craftsman-era Gamble House, occupy grounds on leafy streets. Old Town Pasadena, the historic core, is now home to a vibrant street of restaurants and shops. Pasadena is in the limelight every year on January 1 with its Tournament of Roses, a parade, and football game. The area's other treasures include the Rose Bowl and the fabled Huntington Gardens.

The Rose Bowl, home to the famous annual Tournament of the Roses

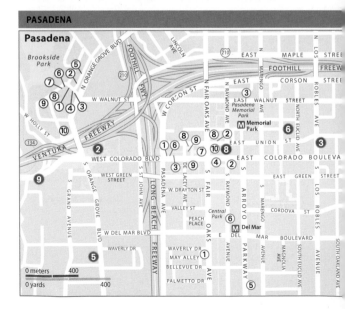

1 Rose Bowl

MAP E1 ■ 1001 Rose Bowl Dr ■ 626-577-3101 ■ www.rosebowl stadium.com

Pasadena's most famous landmark, the Rose Bowl, draws worldwide attention every New Year's Day when two top-ranking college football teams battle it out for the Rose Bowl Game Trophy. College football first became part of the Tournament of Roses in 1902 when Michigan beat Stanford 49–0. The original horseshoe-shaped structure was enlarged to its current capacity of 90,000.

Paintings on display at Norton Simon Museum

2 Norton Simon Museum

MAP E1 ■ 411 W Colorado Blvd ■ 626-449-6840 ■ Open 11am–8pm Fri & Sat, noon–5pm Sun, Mon, Wed & Thu ■ Adm (free for under 19s and students with ID, also on 1st Fri of month) ■ www.nortonsimon.org

This must-see for art lovers owes its existence to Norton Simon, a hugely successful entrepreneur, who collected hundreds of masterpieces *(see p94)* from the Renaissance to the 20th century, and sculptures from India and Southeast Asia. Old Masters, such as Rembrandt and Goya, and the Impressionists, especially Degas, Renoir, Cézanne, and Monet, are well represented. Frank Gehry's remodel improved the lighting of the exhibit space. Sculptures, including Rodin's *The Thinker*, dot the gardens, inspired by Monet's at Giverny in France.

3 Pacific Asia Museum

MAP E1 ■ 46 N Los Robles Ave ■ 626-449-2742 ■ Open 11am–5pm Wed–Sun (until 8pm Thu) ■ Adm (for free entry, check website) ■ www. pacificasiamuseum.usc.edu

Grace Nicholson, infatuated with all things Asian, had her home designed to look like a Chinese imperial palace. It now makes a fitting setting for this museum's 14,000 artifacts from Asia and the Pacific Islands. Exhibits include masks from New Guinea, paintings by Japanese masters Hokusai and Hiroshige, and woven costumes from Pakistan.

4 The Huntington

This treasure trove of culture *(see pp28–31)* is the legacy of railroad tycoon Henry E. Huntington. He made his fortune in real estate and owned LA's first mass transit system.

1 Top 10 Sights
see pp91–3

1 Places to Eat
see p97

1 Shopping in
Old Pasadena
see p96

1 Greene and Greene
Craftsman Houses
see p95

5 Wrigley Mansion and Gardens

MAP E1 ■ 391 S Orange Grove Blvd
■ 602-955-4079 ■ Tours: 10am,
noon, 2pm & 4pm Tue–Sat, 2pm
Sun ($15 per person) ■ www.
wrigleymansionclub.com

William Wrigley Jr., of Wrigley's
chewing gum, certainly knew how
to live. His residence in Pasadena
is an 18,500-sq-ft (1,720-sq-m)
Renaissance-style mansion *(see
p52)*. It houses the Tournament of
Roses Association, which organizes
the annual Rose Bowl Game. Memorabilia includes Rose Queen crowns,
trophies, and photographs.

DOO DAH PARADE

This over-the-top celebration of
wackiness, held every June, began
in 1978 as an irreverent spoof of the
wholesome Rose Parade. Entrants
vary each year, but groups such as
the Synchronized Precision Briefcase
Drill Team and the West Hollywood
Transvestite Cheerleaders always
generate cheers from the 40,000-
strong crowd on Colorado Boulevard.

Wrigley Mansion and Gardens

structures – the Main Library,
the Civic Auditorium, and the
City Hall. Architect Myron Hunt
designed the public library.

6 Pasadena Civic Center

MAP E1 ■ City Hall: 100 N
Garfield Ave, 626-744-4000
■ Civic Auditorium: 300 E Green
St, 626-449-7360 ■ Library: 285 E
Walnut St, 626-744-4052

This grand complex was inspired by
the early 20th-century City Beautiful
movement. It consists of three
European-style Beaux-Arts

7 California Institute of Technology (CalTech)

MAP E2 ■ 1200 E California Blvd
■ 626-395-6811 ■ Campus open
anytime ■ Free guided tours: 10am
Mon–Fri (no tours during the winter
break & on rainy days) ■ www.
caltech.edu

One of the world's leading scientific
research centers and a pioneer in
molecular biology, CalTech counts
29 Nobel Prize winners among its
alumni and faculty, including bio-
logist and current president, David
Baltimore. The institute evolved
from an arts and crafts school
founded in 1891 by the emi-
nent Amos G. Throop,

**City Hall,
Pasadena Civic Center**

hanging its focus to science after astronomer George E. Hale became a board member in 1907.

8 Old Town Pasadena
MAP E2 ∎ Along Colorado Blvd between Marengo Ave & Pasadena Ave ∎ Castle Green, 50 E Green St

Pasadena's historic business district, once a decaying part of town, has now been beautifully restored. Today, its handsome brick buildings are packed with boutiques, restaurants, and bookstores. A short detour will take you to the imposing 1898 Castle Green, once Old Pasadena's most luxurious resort hotel.

9 Colorado Street Bridge
MAP E1 ∎ Court ∎ 125 S Grand Ave

The arches of this restored 1913 bridge straddle the Arroyo Seco (Spanish for "dry brook"), a ravine that starts in the San Gabriel Mountains. The 1903 Vista del Arroyo Hotel overlooking the bridge is home to the Ninth Circuit Court of Appeals. The local historic group throws a block party on the bridge each July.

Colorado Street Bridge

10 Pasadena Playhouse
MAP E1 ∎ 39 S El Molino Ave ∎ 626-356-7529 ∎ Box office: noon–5pm Tue–Sat (until 4pm Sun) ∎ www.pasadenaplayhouse.org

Known as the official state theater of California, it was founded in 1917 and opened in its historic building in 1925. The theater in the round technique was first used here and it has been a center of innovation and a training ground for various artists since. Today it is the center of the Playhouse District of entertainment and shopping.

EXPLORING HISTORIC PASADENA

▶ **MORNING**

A classic way to start the day in Pasadena is with an energizing breakfast at **Marston's** *(see p97)*. After your fill of pancakes, stroll east a couple of blocks on Walnut Street and have a look at the beautiful Beaux-Arts **Main Library** and the majestic **City Hall** a little to the south. Continue walking farther south to Colorado Boulevard, then head west to **Old Town Pasadena**, the city's original Downtown, a popular shopping and dining district. Check out the well-restored historic facades while browsing the stores, then pause briefly for a snack at **Café Santorini** *(see p97)*.

AFTERNOON

In the afternoon, either drive or walk west along Colorado Boulevard, then turn right on Orange Grove Boulevard to catch the 1pm or 2pm tour of the **Gamble House** *(see p95)*, the Craftsman-era magnum opus by Charles and Henry Greene. Fans of this architectural style could check out several more residences designed by the brothers along nearby Arroyo Terrace and Grand Avenue. Alternatively, make your way back to Colorado Boulevard for a visit to the first-rate **Norton Simon Museum** *(see p91)*. The gorgeous gardens are a nice place for some respite and refreshments. A perfect finale to your day is to treat yourself to a grand dinner at **The Raymond** *(see p97)*, one of the city's oldest and most popular restaurants.

See map on pp90–91 ←

Artworks at the Norton Simon Museum

1 Madonna and Child with Book

Renowned renaissance artist Raphael (1483–1520) was only 19 years old when he painted this work. It perfectly exemplifies his geometrically balanced compositions and his ability to imbue his figures with spirituality and great tenderness.

2 Self-Portrait

No artist has left behind such a thorough record of his own likeness as Rembrandt (1606–69). The elegant garb, dapper beret, and gold chain in this portrait emphasize his social status as a sought-after artist.

3 Still Life with Lemons, Oranges, and a Rose

In this still life, Francisco de Zurbarán (1598–1664) applies the bright colors and minute detail usually reserved for his depictions of saints and clergy.

4 The Triumph of Virtue and Nobility Over Ignorance

Rococo master Giovanni Battista Tiepolo (1696–1770) is known for his exuberant ceiling frescoes. This canvas shows off his bold compositions and use of color.

5 Artist's Garden at Vétheuil

Claude Monet (1840–1926) looked out from his house on the Seine at the sunny, flower-filled garden of this painting.

6 Little Dancer Aged Fourteen

Edgar Degas (1834–1917) was fascinated with dancers, and this exquisite sculpture is one of his finest. The figure is partly painted, dressed in a tulle skirt, and has been given real hair.

Portrait of a Peasant by Van Gogh

7 Portrait of a Peasant

Vincent Van Gogh (1853–90) painted Patience Escalier, a gardener and shepherd, against a night-blue background to create "a mysterious effect, like a star in the depths of an azure sky."

8 Exotic Landscape

Henri Rousseau (1844–1910) is renowned for his poetic Naïve paintings that depict lushly landscaped dream worlds. He created this work shortly before his death.

9 Woman with a Book

A highlight of the museum's extensive Picasso (1881–1973) holdings, this graceful painting shows the artist's mistress, Marie-Thérèse Walter, in an introspective mood that contrasts sharply with the melodramatic colors.

10 Shiva and Parvati

This pair of 13th-century Indian bronze sculpture casts depict the Hindu god Shiva, part of the holy Trinity of gods, accompanied by his wife Parvati.

Little Dancer Aged Fourteen by Degas

Craftsman Houses by Greene and Greene

1 Van Rossem-Neill House (1903)

MAP E1 ■ 400 Arroyo Terrace

Hemmed in by an unusual wall made of warped clinker bricks, this pretty house has a stained-glass front door.

2 Cole House (1906)

MAP E1
■ 2 Westmoreland Place

This large home, owned by a church, marks the first time the Greenes added a *porte-cochère* (a porch-like roof) above the driveway.

3 Ranney House (1907)

MAP E1 ■ 440 Arroyo Terrace

Mary Ranney was a draftsperson at the brothers' firm and contributed many of the design ideas for this shingled corner mansion.

4 Hawks House (1906)

MAP E1 ■ 408 Arroyo Terrace

This home is distinguished by a very wide covered porch, which keeps out both heat and light, giving the house a rather sombre appearance.

5 Gamble House (1908)

MAP E1 ■ 4 Westmoreland Place ■ 626-793-3334 ■ Tours noon–3pm Thu–Sun ■ Adm (free for under 12s) ■ www.gamblehouse.org

This handcrafted masterpiece *(see p49)* boasts rich wood, leaded glass windows, and a stained-glass door.

The Gamble House

6 White Sisters House (1903)

MAP E1 ■ 370 Arroyo Terrace

This house has lost much of its Craftsman look due to the replacement of the shingle exterior with painted stucco.

7 Charles Sumner Greene House (1901–16)

MAP E1 ■ 368 Arroyo Terrace

Charles experimented with many Craftsman ideas while building his own home. The front room, buttressed by boulders and bricks, was a later addition.

8 Duncan-Irwin House (1902)

MAP E1 ■ 240 N Grand Ave

This large, beautiful home, originally a single-story bungalow, pays homage to Japanese design with its slightly upturned roofs.

9 James Culbertson House (1902–15)

MAP E1 ■ 235 N Grand Ave

The stained-glass entrance door, the clinker brick wall, and the pergola are the only original elements of this extensively remodeled home.

10 Halsted House (1905)

MAP E1 ■ 90 N Grand Ave

Originally one of the brothers' smallest designs, this bungalow sports a deep overhang of eaves sheltering the main entrance.

See map on pp90–91

Shopping in Old Pasadena

1 Sur La Table
MAP E1 ■ 161 W Colorado Blvd
■ 626-744-9987

Cooking aficionados love browsing through this vast assortment of quality kitchenware, from pots and pans to hard-to-find utensils.

The Distant Lands bookstore

2 Distant Lands Travel Bookstore & Outfitters
MAP E1 ■ 20 S Raymond Ave
■ 626-449-3220

A friendly spot packed with travel books and accessories. There is also a travel agency for tickets and tours.

3 Restoration Hardware
MAP E1 ■ 127 W Colorado Blvd
■ 626-795-7234

This retro emporium specializes in classic furniture and period hardware, but also has a fun selection of trendy home accessories.

4 Lather
MAP E1 ■ 17 E Colorado Blvd
■ 626-396-9636

This "modern apothecary" uses only natural ingredients for its skincare products and has an assortment of olive oil soap sold by weight.

5 Vroman's Bookstore
MAP E1 ■ 695 E Colorado Blvd
■ 626-449-5320

Vroman's has been going strong since 1894, with knowledgeable and helpful staff, author signings, book readings, and an in-house café.

6 Urban Outfitters
MAP E1 ■ 139 W Colorado Blvd
■ 626-449-1818

Hip, urban clothing, vintage outfits, well-known brands, shoes, gifts, and housewares all under one roof.

7 J. Crew
MAP E1 ■ 3 W Colorado Blvd
■ 626-568-2739

The retail store of this famous catalog line has the same stylish clothing and accessories for men and women at reasonable prices.

8 Homage
MAP E1 ■ 2 E Holly St
■ 626-440-7244

From jewelry to small art pieces, cards, unusual gifts and home decor, this shop features local artisans and has rave-worthy gift wrapping paper.

9 Apple Store
MAP E1 ■ 54 W Colorado Blvd
■ 626-577-2685

Everything a Mac enthusiast could want and more. This one-stop shop stocks the latest in Apple technology and has knowledgeable staff.

10 Gold Bug
MAP E1 ■ 22 E Union St
■ 626-744-9963

This unusual boutique stocks a huge assortment of organic jewelry, artworks, home-decor pieces, and nature-based oddities.

Unique artworks at Gold Bug

Places to Eat

PRICE CATEGORIES
Price categories include a three-course
meal for one, a glass of house wine, and all
unavoidable extra charges including tax.

$ under $25 $$ $25–$50 $$$ $50–$80
$$$$ over $80

1 Saladang Garden
MAP E2 ■ 383 S Fair Oaks Ave
■ 626-793-5200 ■ $$

Complex flavors and a lovely Post-
Modern patio make this trendy Thai
eatery a Pasadena favorite.

2 Union Restaurant
MAP E1 ■ 37 E Union St
■ 626-795-5841 ■ $$

Northern Italy meets California
at this intimate neighborhood
restaurant. The small plates –
designed for sharing – are made
from locally sourced ingredients.

3 Marston's
MAP E1 ■ 151 E Walnut St
■ 626-796-2459 ■ Closed Mon ■ $

Start the day with blueberry
pancakes, golden French toast,
or other breakfast favorites at
this popular cottage hangout.

4 The Raymond
MAP E2 ■ 1250 S Fair Oaks Ave
at Columbia St ■ 626-441-3136
■ Closed Mon ■ $$$

This Craftsman-style cottage has a
menu of American classics, but with
limited options for vegetarians.

5 Parkway Grill
MAP E1 ■ 510 S Arroyo
Parkway ■ 626-795-1001 ■ $$$

Only the freshest organic ingredients
are used to perfect Parkway Grill's
inspired Californian cuisine.

6 La Grande Orange Cafe
MAP E1 ■ 260 S Raymond Ave
■ 626-356-4444 ■ $$

Housed in the restored Del Mar
train station (the Gold Line stops
right outside), this family-friendly
restaurant offers a well-prepared,

La Grande Orange Cafe dining area

standard American and Californian-
Mexican menu with an upscale twist.
The charming outdoor patio seating
area is the perfect spot for brunch.

7 Bistro 45
MAP E1 ■ 45 S Mentor Ave
■ 626-795-2478 ■ Closed Mon ■ $$$

This classy place in an Art Deco
building turns out excellent French
fare paired with one of the best wine
lists in town. The menu has limited
options for vegetarians.

8 Café Santorini
MAP E1 ■ 64 W Union St
■ 626-564-4200 ■ $$

The tables on the terrace are the
most coveted on balmy summer
evenings. The Greek and Italian
menu has lots of fun appetizers.

9 Sushi Roku
MAP E1 ■ 33 Miller Alley
■ 626-683-3000 ■ $$$

Classic sushi and creative new takes
on Asian food keep this attractively
designed place busy.

10 Zankou Chicken
MAP E1 ■ 1296 E Colorado Blvd
■ 626-405-1502 ■ $

Armenian eatery specializing in *tarna*
(chicken with hummus, salad, and
garlic sauce), and *shawarma* kebabs.

See map on pp90–91 ←

TOP10 Hollywood

The Hollywood Walk of Fame

Hollywood is at once a town, an industry, and an illusion, and you'll experience all of these along the famed Hollywood Boulevard. Its history encompasses the birth of the movies, the Golden Age of film, and a crushing decline as the studios moved elsewhere. Hollywood has since seen a renaissance along the boulevard – the Hollywood & Highland complex is a major development, and many of the grand movie palaces once again host film openings. At its core, Hollywood is a museum – the huge sign in the hills, the Walk of Fame, the bars that hosted greats such as Ernest Hemingway – this is still the place to rekindle childhood dreams about the "stars."

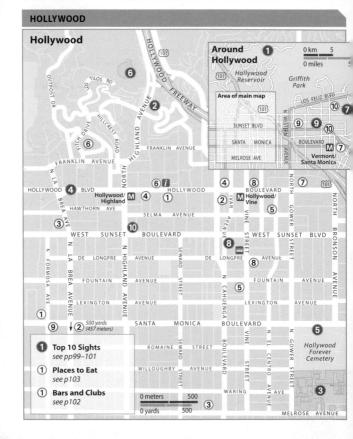

HOLLYWOOD

1 Top 10 Sights
see pp99–101

1 Places to Eat
see p103

1 Bars and Clubs
see p102

1 Hollywood Sign
MAP D2

From the very beginning, the shiny white Hollywood Sign atop Mount Lee was meant to attract attention, originally for the real estate developer and publisher Harry Chandler. Built in 1923 at a cost of $21,000, the sign was once illuminated by 4,000 bulbs and had its own caretaker. Each letter is 50-ft (15-m) tall and is made of sheet metal. In 1932, unemployed actress Peggy Entwistle immortalized herself by leaping to her death off the H. It's illegal to hike to the sign, but the top of Beachwood Drive gets you fairly close.

2 Hollywood Heritage Museum
MAP P1 ▪ 2100 N Highland Ave ▪ 323-874-2276 ▪ Open noon–4pm Sat & Sun ▪ Adm

This museum is housed in the barn where Jesse Lasky and Cecil B. DeMille set up Hollywood's first major film studio in 1913. It was originally located at Selma Avenue and Vine Street, and DeMille shot the first full-length feature *The Squaw Man* here in 1913–14. Exhibits include a re-created studio, photographs, props, and memorabilia from the silent movie era.

3 Paramount Studios
MAP R4 ▪ 5555 Melrose Ave ▪ 323-956-1777 (reservations required) ▪ Adm

The only major movie studio still located in Hollywood, Paramount began making movies with the Paramount logo in 1916. The studio has always turned out classics and, in 1929 its feature *Wings* took home the first ever Best Picture Oscar. Its most successful movies include *Psycho*, *The Godfather*, *Forrest Gump*, and *Titanic*. Two-hour tours of the studio run Monday to Friday.

Paramount Studios entrance

4 Hollywood Boulevard
MAP P2

Hollywood's main artery *(see pp12–13)*, one of the district's most glamorous streets during its pre-World War II heyday, has been revitalized in recent years. The rejuvenation project has focussed on the Hollywood & Highland complex, but old favorites such as TCL Chinese Theatre *(see p63)* and the Walk of Fame have also received a fresh sheen.

Hollywood Boulevard at dusk

Mausoleum of William Andrews Clark Jr. at the Hollywood Forever Cemetery

⑤ Hollywood Forever Cemetery

MAP R3 ■ 6000 Santa Monica Blvd ■ 323-469-1181 ■ Open seasonal hours ■ www.hollywoodforever.com

Founded in 1899, this cemetery is where the famous are buried. The list of those interred here includes Rudolph Valentino, Jane Mansfield, and Cecil B. DeMille. The grandest memorial belongs to Douglas Fairbanks Sr. who, since 2000, has shared his marble tomb with his son, Douglas Jr. A map is available from the nearby flower shop.

Concert at the Hollywood Bowl

⑥ Hollywood Bowl

MAP P1 ■ 2301 N Highland Ave ■ 323-850-2000 ■ Concerts Tue–Sun late Jun–mid-Sep (tickets required) ■ www.hollywoodbowl.com

A night at the world's largest natural amphitheater is as much part of Los Angeles summer tradition as backyard barbecues and fun at the beach. The world's finest artists – from Sinatra to Pavarotti – have performed here since 1922. In 1924, Frank Lloyd Wright designed the first concert shell, improving acoustics.

⑦ Los Feliz and Silver Lake

MAP D2 ■ Ennis House, 2655 Glendower Ave, closed to the public ■ Lovell House, 4616 Dundee Dr, closed to the public ■ Take Red Line to Loz Feliz (Vermont Station)

The twin neighborhoods of Los Feliz and Silver Lake, with their bohemian-chic dining, shopping, and nightlife, constitute one of Los Angeles's oldest movie colonies. The hills are studded with architectural Modernist masterpieces such as Lloyd Wright's 1924 Ennis House and the Lovell House built by Richard Neutra.

HOLLYWOOD SIGN

Over time the Hollywood Sign lost not only its last four letters (it was originally "Hollywoodland") but also its luster, along with the rest of Hollywood. A "save-the-sign" campaign in 1978 received the help of celebrities such as Hugh Hefner, who held a fundraiser, and Alice Cooper, who bought the second O in honor of Groucho Marx.

⑧ Cinerama Dome
MAP Q3 ▪ 323- 464-4226
▪ www.arclightcinemas.com

A Hollywood landmark, this white dome of interlocked triangles is LA's most unusual movie theater. The concrete geodesic dome was built by Welton Beckett in 1963 to show Cinerama movies, a wide-screen technique requiring three 35 mm projectors. The ArcLight theaters (see p62) are also part of the complex.

The interior of Hollyhock House

⑨ Hollyhock House
MAP D2 ▪ 4800 Hollywood Blvd ▪ 323-644-6269 ▪ Tours: 11am–4pm Tue–Sun ▪ Adm (free for under 13s)

The Mayan-style mansion, designed by Lloyd Wright in 1921 for oil heiress Aline Barnsdall, is a community arts center. Depictions of the hollyhock, her favorite flower, appear everywhere on facades and furniture.

⑩ Crossroads of the World
MAP P3 ▪ 6671 Sunset Blvd
▪ Open for strolling

The centerpiece of this unique architectural metaphor is a ship-like Art Deco building that "sails" into a courtyard flanked by cottages in styles ranging from Spanish Colonial to German gingerbread. A quiet office complex, it was built in 1936 by Robert Derrah, who designed the Coca-Coca Bottling Plant (see p81).

A DAY WITH THE STARS

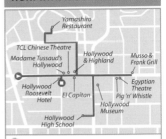

▶ **MORNING**

Begin at La Brea Avenue and Hollywood Boulevard, heading east to the **Hollywood Roosevelt Hotel** (see p12), home of the first Academy Awards. In the **TCL Chinese Theatre** (see p63) you can stand on the footprints of your favorite stars. An escalator will whisk you into the vast **Hollywood & Highland** complex (see p13) with great shopping and views of the **Hollywood Sign** (see p99) and the dazzling **El Capitan** (see p63). Stop by the **Hollywood Museum** (1660 N Highland) to see props, costumes, and sets from film favorites before taking a two-block detour south on Highland Avenue to **Hollywood High School** (1521 N Highland), alma mater of Lawrence Fishburne. Have your picture taken with the stars (almost) at **Madame Tussauds Hollywood** (7024 Hollywood Boulevard). From there, head east for a delicious lunch at **Pig 'n' Whistle** (see p103).

AFTERNOON

Back on Hollywood Boulevard, you'll come across the exotic **Egyptian Theatre** (see p62) and, at No. 6667, **Musso & Frank Grill** (see p103), the oldest restaurant in Hollywood, once the haunt of Chaplin, Hemingway, and other famous people. Wrap up the day with drinks and sunset views at **Yamashiro Restaurant** (see p102), followed by a burger and a Guinness milkshake at the popular and trendy **25 Degrees** at the Hollywood Roosevelt Hotel (7000 Hollywood Blvd).

See map on p98 ⬅

Bars and Clubs

The dimly lit Art Deco-style bar at Boardner's, built in 1942

1 Boardner's
MAP P2 ■ 1652 N Cherokee Ave ■ 323-462-9621 ■ www.boardners.com

This historical bar has a large dance floor and live entertainment.

2 The Room Hollywood
MAP Q2 ■ 1626 N Cahuenga Blvd ■ 866-687-4499 ■ www.theroomhollywood.com

Dance to hip hop, R&B, and occasional old rock at this stylish club with a no-attitude vibe.

3 The Woods
MAP P2 ■ 1533 N La Brea Ave ■ 323-876-6612 ■ www.vintagebargroup.com

Hidden in a nondescript mini-mall, this tiki lounge features live bands.

4 Loaded Hollywood
MAP Q2 ■ 6377 Hollywood Blvd ■ 323-464-5689 ■ www.loadedhollywood.com

A raucous, gritty dive bar that draws hipsters and fashionistas with its strong drinks and loud dance music.

5 Good Times at Davey Wayne's
MAP Q2 ■ 1611 N El Centro Ave ■ 323-962-3804 ■ www.goodtimesatdaveywaynes.com

Tiki drinks and alcohol-infused snow cones are served at this retro bar.

6 Yamashiro Restaurant
MAP P2 ■ 1999 N Sycamore Ave ■ 323-466-5125 ■ www.yamashirorestaurant.com

A spot for sunset drinks with gorgeous city views. Follow with dinner in the Japanese restaurant.

7 Create
MAP Q2 ■ 6021 Hollywood Blvd ■ 323-463-3331 ■ www.createnightclub.com

Top DJs and live electronic music attract large crowds. Tickets sell out early, so call ahead.

8 Frolic Room
MAP Q2 ■ 6245 Hollywood Blvd ■ 323-462-5890

Bartenders wearing bow ties and vests pour the drinks here, while the jukebox entertains.

9 Formosa Café
MAP P3 ■ 7156 Santa Monica Blvd ■ 323-850-9050

Where Humphrey Bogart and Marilyn Monroe once hung out. Enjoy the signature Mai Tais and tasty California-Asian treats.

10 Good Luck Bar
MAP D2 ■ 1514 Hillhurst Ave ■ 323-666-3524

A cool crowd gathers around the oval bar at this fashionable Chinese-style Silver Lake watering hole.

Places to Eat

1 **Jones Hollywood**
MAP N3 ▪ 7205 Santa Monica
Blvd ▪ 323-850-1726 ▪ Closed lunch
Sat & Sun ▪ $$$
Popular with the locals, this little
spot serves classic thin-crust pizza,
spaghetti and meatballs, and for
many, the best apple pie in town.

2 **Franco on Melrose**
MAP N4 ▪ 6919 Melrose Ave
▪ 323-934-3390 ▪ Closed Sun ▪ $$
Enjoy home-made pasta, lamb,
linguine with clams, and *carciofi*
(raw artichoke salad) in the romantic
outside courtyard setting. BYOB.

3 **Providence**
MAP Q4 ▪ 5955 Melrose Ave
▪ 323-460-4170 ▪ $$$
Fresh seafood, tasting menus and
an extensive wine list are the draw at
this elegant, romantic spot *(see p66)*.

Original decor at Pig 'n' Whistle

4 **Pig 'n' Whistle**
MAP P2 ▪ 6714 Hollywood
Blvd ▪ 323-463-0000 ▪ $$
This 1927 landmark has faithfully
retained its gorgeous dark wood
interior. The menu features a
number of famous pork dishes and
has limited options for vegetarians.

PRICE CATEGORIES
Price categories include a three-course
meal for one, a glass of house wine, and all
unavoidable extra charges including tax.

$ under $25 $$ $25–$50 $$$ $50–$80
$$$$ over $80

5 **La Numero Uno**
MAP Q2 ▪ 1247 Vine St
▪ 323-957-1111 ▪ $
A good place for Mexican specialties
such as fried plantain with beans
and cream, and yucca with
chicharrón (fried pork rinds).

6 **The Musso & Frank Grill**
MAP P2 ▪ 6667 Hollywood
Blvd ▪ 323-467-7788 ▪ $$
Steaks and chops dominate the menu
of Hollywood's oldest restaurant (open
since 1919). It was a major hangout
for celebrities such as Hemingway.

7 **Café Stella**
MAP D2 ▪ 3932 W Sunset Blvd
▪ 323-666-0265 ▪ Closed Sun & Mon
▪ $$
This romantic French-style eatery
offers mostly outdoor seating in a
lovely courtyard with hanging amber
lights and olive and lavender plants.

8 **Los Balcones del Peru**
MAP Q3 ▪ 1360 Vine St
▪ 323-871-9600 ▪ $$
This is a casual spot for delicious
Peruvian food. Wash it all down with
Argentinian wine or Peruvian beer.

9 **Jitlada Restaurant**
MAP D2 ▪ 5233 W Sunset Blvd
▪ 323-667-9809 ▪ Closed Mon ▪ $$
Considered by many to be the best
Thai in LA, Jitlada serves up exotic
curries and delightful papaya salads.

10 **Yuca's Hut**
MAP D2 ▪ 2056 Hillhurst Ave,
Los Feliz ▪ 323-662-1214 ▪ Closed
Sun ▪ No credit cards ▪ $
Head this way for yummy Mexican
food. Try the *cochinita pibil* tacos. Only
non-vegetarian food is served here.

See map on p98

TOP 10 West Hollywood and Midtown

West Hollywood is LA's party zone and teems with nightclubs, restaurants, bars, and comedy clubs. After dark, Sunset Strip is the center of the action for poseurs, producers, and the pretty in-crowd. This is also LA's gay quarter, especially along Santa Monica Boulevard. For shopaholics there's Melrose Avenue, a quirky pathway lined with designer stores, tattoo parlors, Gothic-chic shops, and bustling cafés and eateries. It's also home to the Pacific Design Center, the anchor of the Avenues of Art & Design. For cultural edification, head south to an amorphous district we've termed "Midtown," whose main artery, Wilshire Boulevard, boasts some of the city's finest museums along the historic Miracle Mile.

Historic trolley on The Grove

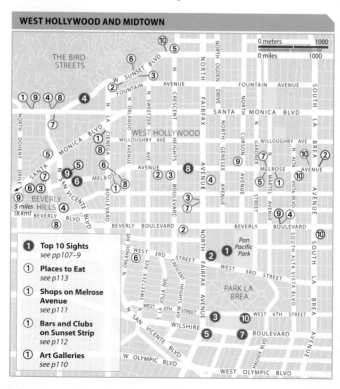

WEST HOLLYWOOD AND MIDTOWN

1 Top 10 Sights
see pp107–9

1 Places to Eat
see p113

1 Shops on Melrose Avenue
see p111

1 Bars and Clubs on Sunset Strip
see p112

1 Art Galleries
see p110

Previous pages Campus of the University of California, Los Angeles

1 The Grove

MAP N5 ■ 189 The Grove Drive
■ 323-900-8000 ■ Open 10am–9pm
Mon–Thu, 10am–10pm Fri & Sat,
10am–8pm Sun

Adjoining the Farmers Market, the
Grove is an attractive, upscale
outdoor shopping and dining center
with a first-rate 14-screen movie
theater. This mall features highlights
such as a historic trolley and a
fountain with a water show set to
music. Along with adjacent CBS
Television City and the Farmers
Market, the Grove occupies land
once owned by the Gilmore family.
Gilmore Stadium, home of the
Hollywood Stars, a baseball team
owned by Bing Crosby, Cecil B.
DeMille, and Barbara Stanwyck, was
once located where CBS now stands.

2 Original Farmers Market

MAP M5 ■ 6333 W 3rd St
■ 323-954-4230 ■ Open 9am–9pm
Mon–Fri, 9am–8pm Sat, 10am–7pm
Sun ■ www.farmersmarketla.com

In 1934, two entrepreneurs asked
landowner E. B. Gilmore for per-
mission to start a produce market
on a vacant parking lot on his
property. Soon after, a group
of farmers started selling fresh
fruit, flowers, and vegetables
from trucks. Many of the 150
stalls of Farmers Market,
such as Magee's Nuts, have
been in the same families
for generations. Scouts from
nearby CBS TV City roam in
search of game-show
audience members.

Farmers Market

Twelve Months of the Year, **LACMA**

3 Los Angeles County Museum of Art (LACMA)

A virtual cornucopia of paintings,
sculpture, furniture, and objects that
would take several days to peruse
await in six buildings. LACMA *(see
pp20–23)* also hosts touring exhibits.

4 Sunset Strip

Sunset Strip has been LA's
nocturnal playground since the
1920s and is the most history-
laden section of the 25-mile
(40-km) Sunset Boulevard.
With redevelopment under-
way, new hotels and clubs
are set to open in 2019
and 2020. Landmarks
including the Chateau
Marmont, the Whisky a
Go-Go, the Mondrian Hotel
with its exclusive SkyBar,
and the Viper Room music
club *(see pp14–15)*, still
attract stars and fans.

Futuristic building of the Petersen Automotive Museum

5 Petersen Automotive Museum

MAP M6 ■ 6060 Wilshire Blvd, Miracle Mile ■ 323-930-2277 ■ Open 6am–11pm daily ■ Adm

LA's evolution from sleepy outpost to sweeping megalopolis is uniquely tied to the rise of the automobile. This is the basic premise of this wonderful museum, which does a lot more than display pretty vintage cars (though there are plenty of those, too). On the ground floor, you'll follow a Los Angeles "streetscape" through 100 years of car history. You'll pass dioramas of a 1920s gas station, a 1930s show-room, and a 1950s drive-in restaurant. Upstairs, the cars take center stage. Exhibits change regularly, but they usually include galleries devoted to hot rods, motorcycles, and vehicles owned by celebrities or used in movies. For children, the Discovery Center makes science fun.

6 Avenues of Art & Design

MAP L4 ■ Along Beverly Blvd, Robertson Blvd, & Melrose Ave between La Cienega Blvd & Doheny Dr

The streets surrounding the Pacific Design Center (PDC) are flanked with design stores where you can actually buy – and not just look at (as in the PDC) – what you see. Best explored on foot, the district is filled with cutting-edge art galleries (see p110), trendy restaurants, and cafés.

7 Craft & Folk Art Museum (CAFAM)

MAP N6 ■ 5814 Wilshire Blvd, Miracle Mile ■ 323-937-4230 ■ Open 11am–5pm Tue–Fri, 11am–6pm Sat & Sun 6:30–9:30pm first Thu of month ■ Adm (free for under 10s) ■ www.cafam.org

This small museum is dedicated to showcasing handicrafts and folk art from around the world. The brain-child of folk art collector Edith Wyle, it was originally launched in 1965 as "The Egg and The Eye," a gallery space and omelet restaurant. Apart from its changing exhibits, CAFAM is best known for its annual International Festival of Masks, which is held in October.

8 Melrose Avenue

Though it has seen better days, Melrose Avenue (see p111) is still a haven for Hollywood hipsters and the place to stock up on vintage threads, provocative fashions, and unusual gift items. Weekend after-noons are prime time for soaking it all up.

Fashion from Melrose Avenue

GAY LOS ANGELES

West Hollywood is the center of LA's gay and lesbian community. There's plenty of partying in the many happening bars, clubs, cafés, and restaurants along Santa Monica Boulevard. Huge crowds turn up for the colorful Christopher Street West Parade in June and the wonderfully outrageous Halloween Carnival.

⑨ Pacific Design Center (PDC)

MAP L4 ■ 8687 Melrose Ave, 310-657-0800, open 9am–5pm Mon–Fri ■ MOCA at PDC: 310-289-5223, open 11am–5pm Tue–Fri (to 8pm Thu), 11am–6pm Sat & Sun ■ www.moca.org

The 130 showrooms of this complex display the finest in furniture, fabrics, lighting, and accessories. With a contemporary 1975 design by Cesar Pelli the most striking feature of the PDC is the blue glass facade, known as "The Blue Whale." The clover-green addition dates from 1988. Behind the PDC is a branch of the Museum of Contemporary Art (see p78), showcasing architecture and design.

Page Museum entrance

⑩ Page Museum at the La Brea Tar Pits

MAP N6 ■ 5801 Wilshire Blvd, Miracle Mile ■ 323-934-7243 ■ Open 9:30am–5:30pm ■ Adm (free first Tue of the month, every Tue in Sep, and for under 5s) ■ www.tarpits.org

Mammoths, saber-toothed cats, and dire wolves are the stars of this museum offering a look at life in LA during the last Ice Age. Since 1906, excavations at the pits adjacent to the museum have yielded over a million fossilized bones of about 450 species of insects, birds and mammals. Many are now on display here. There is also a glass-walled laboratory where paleontologists may be seen working. Outside the museum, life-size replicas of mammoths trapped in muck dramatize the ghastly fate of Los Angeles's prehistoric denizens.

A DAY IN HOLLYWOOD

▶ MORNING

Start your day at Wilshire Boulevard's "Museum Row" to catch the latest headline exhibit at **LACMA** (see pp20–23) or to see selections from its superb permanent collection. Don't miss the beautiful Pavilion for Japanese Art. If you can muster the energy before lunch, head to the **Petersen Automotive Museum** or the **Page Museum**.

Leaving Museum Row, drive a few blocks north to the **Farmers Market** (see p107), and try the Cajun food at Gumbo Pot, or the all-American menu at Du-Par's.

AFTERNOON

For an afternoon of shopping, start with the Farmers Market itself, then wander over to **The Grove** (see p107), an outdoor mall. Head north on Fairfax Avenue, turning right on **Melrose Avenue**. This quintessential LA shopping street is packed with fun and funky stores and offers great people-watching opportunities, especially on weekends.

Head off for an early dinner at **Lucques** (see p113), with its delicious Californian-Mediterranean cuisine, then drive up to **Sunset Strip** (see p107) for an evening of laughs at the **Comedy Store** (see p65) or **The Laugh Factory** (see p65). Make your reservations in advance. Showtime is usually 8pm. Round off your day with a drink at **Bar Marmont** (see p112) or the lounge at the chic **Standard Hollywood** (see p146).

See map on p106 ←

Art Galleries

1 Morán Morán
MAP L4 ▪ 937 N La Cienega Blvd ▪ 310-652-1711

A spacious gallery exhibiting trendsetting contemporary work by several artists, including the late photographer Robert Mapplethorpe.

2 Gallery 1988
MAP K4 ▪ 7021 Melrose Ave ▪ 323-937-7088

This small space is crowded with some of the city's hottest new talent. It is known as the best place in the US for pop-culture-themed work.

3 George Stern Fine Arts
MAP K4 ▪ 8920 Melrose Ave ▪ 310-276-2600

This gallery specializes in late 19th- and early 20th-century Impressionist landscape painters based in California such as Guy Rose.

4 Leica Store and Gallery
MAP L5 ▪ 8783 Beverly Blvd ▪ 424-777-0341

In addition to a sales showroom of Leica cameras, a gallery celebrates the world through the lenses of the world's finest photographers.

5 Hamilton-Selway Fine Art Gallery
MAP L4 ▪ 8678 Melrose Ave ▪ 310-657-1711

Home to the largest collection of Andy Warhol originals on the West Coast, this gallery also features Roy Lichtenstein, Keith Haring, and other pop art icons.

6 Louis Stern Fine Arts
MAP M4 ▪ 9002 Melrose Ave ▪ 310-276-0147

Mid-century abstract artists from the West Coast are featured in this gallery. It also acts as an agent for private parties selling impressionist, modern and Latin American art.

7 101/EXHIBIT
MAP K4 ▪ 8920 Melrose Ave ▪ 310-271-7980

The works of established as well as up-and-coming contemporary artists are featured at this innovative gallery.

8 Gallery 825
MAP L3 ▪ 825 La Cienega Blvd ▪ 310-652-8272

Owned by the Los Angeles Art Association, it has four exhibit areas showing works by its cooperative members. All genres are represented, with a focus on contemporary art.

9 Tobey C. Moss
MAP N5 ▪ 7321 Beverly Blvd ▪ 323-933-5523

This LA art-scene fixture began with a focus on prints and drawings, but is best known as a keen promoter of pre-1960s California Modernists.

10 Fahey/Klein Gallery
MAP P5 ▪ 148 N La Brea Ave ▪ 323-934-2250

A power in the world of rare, vintage, and contemporary art photography, Fahey/Klein showcases Henri Cartier-Bresson and other high-profile artists.

Fine art photography exhibition at Fahey/Klein Gallery

Shops on Melrose Avenue

Jewelry galore at Maya Jewelry

(1) Maya Jewelry
MAP N4 ■ 7360 Melrose Ave
■ 323-655-2708

This small store stocks affordable jewelry, mostly silver, to adorn any body part you wish. It also has a great mask collection.

(2) Decades & Decades Two
MAP M4 ■ 8214 Melrose Ave
■ 323-655-1960

If Rodeo Drive is out of your league, try this couture resale boutique that stocks second-hand clothing and 1960s and 1970s Pucci and Courrèges.

(3) Fred Segal
MAP M4 ■ 8100 Melrose Ave (also at 420 Broadway, 500 Broadway)
■ 323-651-4129, 310-394-9814

This über-trendy house of style (see p54) attracts A-list celebrities. Shop for luxurious clothes, beauty products, and gift items at steep prices.

(4) Melrose Trading Post
MAP M4 ■ At the corner of Melrose & Fairfax aves ■ 323-655-7679 ■ Open 9am–5pm Sun ■ Adm (free for under 12s)

This cool Sunday flea market takes you back through the years with vintage fashions, collectibles, and retro furnishings.

(5) Wasteland
MAP N4 ■ 7428 Melrose Ave
■ 323-653-3028

Stylists and bargain-hunters shop for vintage clothing, accessories, and shoes at this warehouse-sized store.

(6) Wanna Buy a Watch?
MAP N4 ■ 8465 Melrose Ave
■ 323-653-0467

Best known for its selection of vintage watches, this classy store now also stocks contemporary watch models, antique diamond rings, and 1920s Art Nouveau baubles.

(7) l.a.Eyeworks
MAP N4 ■ 7407 Melrose Ave
■ 323-653-8255

This unusual and vibrant store is known for featuring the most unique eyeglass designs on the planet and attracts its share of the hip crowd.

(8) Kelly Wearstler
MAP L4 ■ 8440 Melrose Ave
■ 323-895-7880

A favorite destination for celebrity shoppers, this lifestyle store stocks home décor, furniture, lighting, fabrics, and gifts.

Jewelry box, Kelly Wearstler

(9) Flasher
MAP N4 ■ 7609 Melrose Ave ■ 323-655-3375

Stylist and owner Scott specializes in flashy statement pieces for men and women looking to stand out in the club scene or those who just want to add an artistic, urban edge to their wardrobes.

(10) Necromance
MAP P4 ■ 7220 Melrose Ave
■ 323-934-8684

If the sight of freeze-dried ducklings gives you the creeps, you should probably avoid this "little shop of horrors." Budding sorcerers will find delightfully macabre stuff to buy.

See map on p106

Bars and Clubs on Sunset Strip

1 Rainbow Bar & Grill
MAP K3 ■ 9015 Sunset Blvd
■ 310-278-4232

Rock'n'roll devotees flock to this legendary bar filled with photos, records, and guitars of every headliner rocker group imaginable.

Upscale SkyBar, with its famous pool

2 SkyBar
MAP M3 ■ 8440 Sunset Blvd, at the Mondrian Hotel ■ 323-848-6025

Famous for its poolside cocktails, celebrity crowd, and sweeping city views. Getting past the velvet rope here is a tall order.

3 The Cactus Lounge at the Standard
MAP M3 ■ 8300 Sunset Blvd
■ 323-822-3111

The entertainment at this hotel hot spot includes a live acoustic music series, book readings, a DJ above the reception, and dancing.

4 Pearl's Rooftop
MAP L3 ■ 8909 Sunset Blvd
■ 310-360-6800

Resembling a 1920s-style speakeasy, Pearl's has three levels of drinking fun, including an upper deck with views across West Hollywood.

5 Hyde Sunset Kitchen & Cocktails
MAP M3 ■ 8117 Sunset Blvd
■ 323-940-1650

Expect exclusivity and attitude at this celeb-heavy nightclub, with private tables and large couches.

6 Saddle Ranch Chop House
MAP M3 ■ 8371 W Sunset Blvd
■ 323-656-2007

A Texas-style steakhouse popular with families until 10pm, when it becomes a lively night-time hangout.

7 The Viper Room
MAP L3 ■ 8852 Sunset Blvd
■ 310-358-1880

Celebrity musicians such as Bruce Springsteen stage concerts (see p54) at this famous club (see p15).

8 Whisky a Go-Go
MAP L3 ■ 8901 W Sunset Blvd
■ 310-652-4202

LA's epicenter of rock'n'roll in the 1960s, this club found fame for The Doors and still books new bands.

9 The Roxy
MAP K3 ■ 9009 W Sunset Blvd
■ 310-278-9457

This no-nonsense club is loved by serious fans as its focus is on the show, not the decor or the crowd.

10 Bar Marmont
MAP M3 ■ 8171 Sunset Blvd
■ 323-650-0575

Super-trendy lounge next to the Chateau Marmont hotel (see p145) with lots of beautiful people. To increase your chances of getting past the front door arrive early, by about 9 or 10pm.

Neon signs at Bar Marmont

Places to Eat

Alfresco dining at Lucques

PRICE CATEGORIES
Price categories include a three-course meal for one, a glass of house wine, and all unavoidable extra charges including tax.

$ under $25 $$ $25–$50 $$$ $50–$80
$$$$ over $80

1 Lucques
MAP N4 ▪ 8474 Melrose Ave
▪ 323-655-6277 ▪ $$$$

Try the pancetta-wrapped trout at this intimate spot, then enjoy the desserts by the fireplace.

2 Swingers
MAP M5 ▪ 8020 Beverly Blvd
▪ 323-653-5858 ▪ $$

This retro diner with its plaid booths and Andy Warhol wallpaper serves steamy chicken soup and bulging sandwiches until the wee hours.

3 Animal
MAP M4 ▪ 435 N Fairfax
▪ 323-782-9225 ▪ $$$

Animal serves rich, indulgent, and carnivore-friendly food. Try the chicken-liver mousse.

4 Angelini Osteria
MAP N5 ▪ 7313 Beverly Blvd
▪ 323-297-0070 ▪ Veg: On request
▪ Closed Mon ▪ $$$

Having cooked for the Pope and presidents, Chef Angelini now delights foodies with his comfort food.

5 Guisados
MAP L4 ▪ 8935 Santa Monica
Blvd ▪ 310-777-0310 ▪ $

A variety of tasty meats topped on corn tortillas are served here.

6 Joan's on Third
MAP M5 ▪ 8350 W 3rd St
▪ 323-655-2285 ▪ $

This little deli is great for gourmets on the go or out for a casual lunch. The tarragon chicken salad is great.

7 Canter's Deli
MAP M4 ▪ 419 N Fairfax
▪ 323-651-2030 ▪ $$

An LA classic since 1931, this family-owned Jewish style deli is a popular after-hours spot.

8 The Ivy
MAP L4 ▪ 113 N Robertson
Blvd ▪ 310-274-8303 ▪ $$$

Join the stars in two dining rooms filled with flowers. Try the Caesar salad or the crispy crab cakes.

Floral decorations at The Ivy

9 Echigo
MAP R3 ▪ 12217 Santa Monica
Blvd ▪ 310-820-9787 ▪ Closed Sun
▪ $$$

Sushi of all types and stripes is on offer, and all of it is fresh.

10 M Café de Chaya
MAP P4 ▪ 7119 Melrose Ave
▪ 323-525-0588 ▪ $$

Chaya's macrobiotic cuisine has a huge following. Try the exquisite club sandwich with tempeh "bacon."

See map on p106

TOP 10 Beverly Hills, Westwood, and Bel-Air

Staff in livery standing over rows of Rolls-Royces, Tom Cruise disembarking from a stretch limo, cellphone-addicted fat-cat producers cutting poolside deals in pleasure-palace hotels – this is Beverly Hills, where the smell of money pervades. Adjacent Westwood is home to UCLA, one of the finest universities in the country. Bel Air mansions have routinely passed from Fairbanks and Bogart to Streisand and Diaz. The nearby Getty Center serenely lords above it all in its white majesty.

The iconic Beverly Hills Hotel

① Beverly Hills Hotel
MAP J4 ■ 9641 Sunset Blvd ■ 310-276-2251 ■ www.beverlyhills hotel.com

LA's most famous hotel (see p146) has been part of Hollywood history since its 1912 opening. Douglas Fairbanks Sr. and Will Rogers got drunk in the bar, Howard Hughes rented Bungalow 3 for 30 years, and Marilyn Monroe reportedly romanced both JFK and RFK here. Political leaders, royals, and film stars have all stayed, partied, and cavorted at the legendary Pink Palace.

BEVERLY HILLS, WESTWOOD, AND BEL-AIR

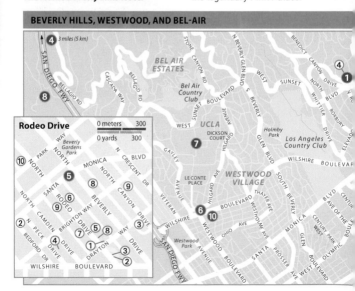

Upscale designer boutiques line Rodeo Drive

2 Rodeo Drive

Rodeo Drive *(see p68)* is one of the world's most famous – and expensive – shopping streets, synonymous with a lifestyle of luxury and fame. Only three blocks long, it is essentially a haute couture runway, with all the major international players represented here *(see p118)*. You'll often spot nicely groomed shoppers, although actual star sightings are rare. Rodeo's southern end is punctuated by the Beverly Wilshire *(see p144)*, one of LA's grandest hotels. Architecture fans should check out Frank Lloyd Wright's Anderton Court *(see p118)*.

3 Beverly Hills Civic Center

MAP J5 ▪ East of Crescent Dr between Santa Monica Blvd & Burton Dr

The wealth of a city is often reflected in its public buildings, so it should come as no surprise that Beverly Hills' civic center is the envy of other towns. The elegant City Hall was built in 1932 in Spanish Renaissance style and harmoniously incorporated into a contemporary Spanish-style complex with palm-lined walkways and curved colonnades. It houses a beautiful library.

4 Skirball Cultural Center

MAP C2 ▪ 2701 N Sepulveda Blvd, Brentwood/Bel-Air ▪ 310-440-4500 ▪ Open noon–5pm Tue–Fri, 10am–5pm Sat & Sun ▪ Adm (free for under 2s, free Thu) ▪ www.skirball.org

This modern Jewish cultural center was named after benefactor Jack Skirball (1896–1985), a rabbi and producer of Hitchcock films. The complex hosts live events and has a multimedia museum. Exhibits explore the parallels between the Jewish experience and the principles of American democracy. The ongoing exhibition, *Visions and Values*, looks at Jewish life from Antiquity to America.

1 Top 10 Sights
see pp114–17

1 Places to Eat
see p119

1 Temptations on Rodeo Drive
see p118

5 The Paley Center for Media

MAP J5 ▪ 465 N Beverly Dr ▪ 310-786-1000 ▪ Open noon–5pm Wed–Sun ▪ Donation ▪ www.paleycenter.org

Most people alive today have grown up watching television, one of the defining media of the 20th century. This center, housed in a striking building by Getty Center architect Richard Meier, was originally built to collect, preserve, and share nearly 80 years of radio and TV history. About 120,000 programs – from news to musicals and sports to sitcoms – have been cataloged and are available for viewing and listening. Today it has expanded to include resources for digital media and offers a wide schedule of classes and events.

Exhibition, UCLA Hammer Museum

6 UCLA Hammer Museum

MAP C2 ▪ 10899 Wilshire Blvd ▪ 310-443-7000 ▪ Open 11am–8pm Tue–Fri, 11am–5pm Sat & Sun ▪ Adm (free: for under 17s, for students with ID, Thu) ▪ www.hammer.ucla.edu

This museum, run by UCLA, is the legacy of Armand Hammer, an oil tycoon who discovered a passion for collecting art in the 1920s. Hammer was especially fond of 19th-century French Impressionists such as Monet. Rotating exhibitions are complemented by traveling shows with a more contemporary angle. Free readings, film screenings, and lectures are quite popular. Phone ahead or check the website for the latest events and exhibits.

Royce Hall entrance, UCLA

7 University of California, Los Angeles (UCLA)

MAP C2 ▪ 310-825-4321 ▪ www.ucla.edu

One of the nation's top research universities, UCLA (founded in 1919) counts many luminaries among its alumni, including Francis Ford Coppola. It has around 150 buildings, with architectural gems such as Royce Hall. The Fowler Museum has a marvellous collection of non-Western art. To the north is the lovely Franklin D. Murphy Sculpture Garden (see p53).

8 The Getty Center

Although best known for its collection of European art, the Getty (see pp16–19) offers much more – a hilltop setting with sweeping views from the ocean to the mountains,

CITY OF CONTRASTS

Out of the nation's largest metro areas, Los Angeles ranks seventh in income inequality. A study infers that this high rate of inequality threatens the region's long-term economic well-being. Both middle-wage and low-wage jobs have declined at a high rate, and the city's neighborhoods are becoming increasingly segregated by race and income.

architecture as exquisite as "frozen music" (to quote Goethe), and landscaped gardens that are nothing less than the finest art.

9 Museum of Tolerance
MAP D2 ■ 9786 W Pico Blvd ■ 310-772-2505 ■ Open 10am–5pm Sun–Fri (Nov–Mar: until 3pm Fri) ■ Closed Jewish holidays ■ Reservations advised ■ Adm ■ www.museumoftolerance.com

This high-tech museum, the only museum of its kind in the world, confronts visitors with issues of extreme intolerance to make them realize the need for greater acceptance in today's world. The experience begins at the "Tolerancenter," whose exhibits address issues such as human-rights violations and the Civil Rights movement. The Holocaust section, at the core, chronicles Nazi atrocities. An interesting multimedia exhibit follows the lives of well-known Americans from different ethnic backgrounds.

Marilyn Monroe's epitaph, Westwood

10 Pierce Brothers Westwood Village Memorial Park
MAP C2 ■ 1218 Glendon Ave ■ 310-474-1579 ■ Open 8am–sunset

This small cemetery beneath Westwood's office high-rises has more stars per square yard than any other in LA. Marilyn Monroe's remains rest in an above-ground crypt that is always decorated with flowers (Hugh Hefner had allegedly reserved the adjacent space). Other celebs buried here are Natalie Wood, Burt Lancaster, and Frank Zappa.

A TOUR OF STARS' HOMES

▶ MORNING

Begin your tour of stars' homes by driving north on **Walden Drive**, just off Santa Monica Boulevard, for a glimpse of the "**Witch's House**", located at the corner of Carmelita Avenue and famous for its Hansel and Gretel looks. Go right on Lomitas Avenue, then left on Linden Drive, where mobster Bugsy Siegel was gunned down at **No. 810** in 1947. Follow Linden north to Sunset Boulevard, turn right, then left on Roxbury Drive for two star-packed blocks. As well as Jimmy Stewart's former home at **No. 918**, you'll see the erstwhile homes of song lyricist Ira Gershwin (**No. 1021**), Diane Keaton (**No. 1025**), singer Rosemary Clooney (aunt of George, at **No. 1019**), Peter Falk (**No. 1004**), comedian Jack Benny (**No. 1002**), and Lucille Ball (**No. 1000**).

Turn right on Canyon Drive, then right again on Bedford Drive, where the house at **No. 904** was at different times the home of stars such as Frank Sinatra, Rex Harrison, Anthony Quinn, Greta Garbo and Ava Gardner. Steve Martin used to live at **No. 721** and Lana Turner at **No. 730**. It was here in 1958 that Lana's daughter Cheryl Crane is believed to have killed her mother's mobster-lover Johnny Stompanato. **No. 512** is the former home of silent screen siren Clara Bow – where, in 1927, she was rumored to have "entertained" the entire USC football team, including Marion Morrison, better known by his screen name of John Wayne.

See map on pp114–15 ←

Temptations on Rodeo Drive

Bijan's two branded luxury cars parked outside the exclusive boutique

1 Two Rodeo
MAP J6 ■ Rodeo Dr at Wilshire Blvd

This cobbled lane resembles an idealized European shopping avenue with fountains and a piazza. When it opened in 1990, it was the first new street in Beverly Hills since 1914.

2 Tiffany & Co
MAP J5 ■ 210 N Rodeo Dr
■ 310-273-8880

The meticulously crafted jewelry is as exquisite as Audrey Hepburn was in the movie *Breakfast at Tiffany's*, based on the store in New York.

3 Lalique
MAP J5 ■ 238 N Rodeo Dr
■ 310-271-7892

Best known for its exquisite crystal pieces, this boutique also stocks jewelry, watches, and perfume.

4 Louis Vuitton
MAP J5 ■ 295 N Rodeo Dr
■ 310-859-0457

Known for its luxury signature leather goods, it also stocks fragrances, fine watches, jewelry and made-to-order shoes.

5 Anderton Court
MAP J5 ■ 333 N Rodeo Dr

One of Frank Lloyd Wright's later buildings (1953), the zigzagging ramp around a well of light is reminiscent of New York's Guggenheim Museum.

6 Bijan
MAP J5 ■ 420 N Rodeo Dr
■ 310-273-6544 ■ By appointment only

This boutique stocks quality menswear which is said to be the world's most expensive. Famous client names are etched into the window.

7 Gucci
MAP J5 ■ 347 N Rodeo Dr
■ 310-278-3451

The store is a sure-fire winner in the looks department, but most customers have eyes only for the trademark shoes and handbags.

8 Harry Winston
MAP J5 ■ 310 N Rodeo Dr
■ 310-271-8554

On Oscar night, when the stars come out in their diamonds, they're most likely on loan from here, one of the world's most exclusive jewelers.

9 The Rodeo Collection
MAP J5 ■ 421 N Rodeo Dr

A white marble outdoor shopping mall with five floors of boutiques orbiting a sunken atrium courtyard with a fancy eatery.

10 O'Neill House
MAP J5 ■ 507 N Rodeo Dr
■ Not open to the public

This 1988 complex sports whimsical Art Nouveau design elements borrowed from architect Gaudí.

Places to Eat

1 Spago Beverly Hills
MAP K5 ■ 176 N Canon Dr
■ 310-385-0880 ■ $$$$

Stargazers are likely to report sightings when dining at Wolfgang Puck's flagship restaurant *(see p67)*.

2 Crustacean
MAP J5 ■ 9646 S Santa Monica Blvd ■ 310-205-8990 ■ $$$

A Beverly Hills hot spot, this serves refined Vietnamese cuisine. Try anything made with owner/chef's "secret spices."

3 The Palm
MAP K5 ■ 267 N Canon Dr
■ 310-550-8811 ■ $$$$

This classic steakhouse is noted for its excellent service and caricatures of the stars that line the walls. Start out with the crab cakes, but save room for the generous deserts.

Courtyard dining at the Polo Lounge

4 Polo Lounge
MAP J4 ■ 9641 Sunset Blvd
■ 310-276-2251 ■ $$$$

This restaurant mixes signature dishes such as McCarthy salad with Asian and Californian cuisine. Vegetarian options available on request.

5 Belvedere
MAP J5 ■ 9882 Santa Monica Blvd ■ 310-788-2306 ■ $$$

Hollywood power brokers love the gold and peach dining room and

impeccable service here. The menu changes with the seasons to make the most of local produce.

6 Maude
MAP ■ 212 S Beverly Dr
■ 310-859-3418 ■ $$$$

A new tasting menu every three months highlights seasonal specialties inspired by the world's leading wine regions. Reservations are a must for this cozy restaurant *(see p67)*.

7 Matsuhisa
MAP L5 ■ 129 N La Cienega Blvd ■ 310-659-9639 ■ $$$

This is the original of Nobu Matsuhisa's small but growing empire of Japanese-Peruvian seafood restaurants. Ignore the menu and surrender to the chef's formidable imagination.

8 Nate'n Al
MAP J5 ■ 414 N Beverly Dr
■ 310-274-0101 ■ $

This modest kosher deli has been catering to the stars since 1943. Regulars swear by the huge sandwiches served on chunky rye bread.

9 Xi'an
MAP J5 ■ 362 N Canon Dr
■ 310-275-3345 ■ $$

For a light and tasty take on classic Chinese dishes, head to this stylish place with an outdoor patio. Try the marvelous black bean sauce and the Peking duck.

10 Il Cielo
MAP K5 ■ 9018 Burton Way
■ 310-276-9990 ■ Closed Sun ■ $$$

Book a romantic table beneath a starlit sky in the enchanting garden and enjoy the classic Italian fare.

See map on pp114–15

TOP10 Santa Monica Bay

Detail, Malibu Adamson House

Santa Monica Bay spans 20 miles (32 km) between two of the richest communities in California – Malibu and Palos Verdes. It's truly the "Gold Coast" of the Golden State, and its shores have some of the finest beaches anywhere, including Topanga, Santa Monica, and Venice on through Manhattan, Hermosa, Redondo, and Torrance. American surfing, and the youth culture it spawned, was born here. In the movies, these fabled beaches have stood in for everything from Guadalcanal and Tahiti to Shangri-la. The rows of huge, stately palms along the Santa Monica promenade cliffs epitomize California.

The main attraction, however, is Santa Monica Pier, which offers sundry entertainment options and a lively carnival atmosphere.

SANTA MONICA BAY

Santa Monica Bay
Calabasa
Studio City
Cornell
Malibu Creek State Park
Topanga State Park
Monte Nido
Beverly Hills
Malibu
Malibu Adamson House
Point Dume
Santa Monica
see Santa Monica map, right
Marina del Rey
Inglewood
Los Angeles
El Segundo
Hawthorne
Pacific Ocean
South Bay
Redondo Beach
Torrance
Palos Verdes Peninsula
Wayfarer's Chapel

7 miles (11 km)

1 **Top 10 Sights**
see pp121–3

1 **Places to Eat**
see p127

1 **Unique Main Street Boutiques**
see p125

1 **Venice Boardwalk Attractions**
see p124

1 **Outdoor Pursuits**
see p126

0 km   5
0 miles   5

1 Malibu Adamson House

MAP B2 ▪ 23200 Pacific Coast Hwy, Malibu, 310-456-8432 ▪ Malibu Lagoon Museum: open 11am–3pm; adm (free for under 18s) ▪ Adamson House: open 11am–2pm Wed–Sat; adm (cash only)

Overlooking the Malibu Lagoon, this Spanish Colonial-style mansion was built by Rhoda Rindge Adamson and her husband Merritt in 1928. The complex showcases hand-painted ceramic tiles manufactured by Malibu Potteries, owned by the Rindge family. The Rindges also built the Malibu Colony, a celebrity enclave where Tom Hanks has a house. The Malibu Lagoon Museum next to the Adamson House chronicles Malibu's history, from its Chumash Indian origins to its position as movie star Shangri-la.

2 Third Street Promenade

MAP B3 ▪ 3rd St between Broadway & Wilshire Blvd, Santa Monica

Downtown Santa Monica's main artery, this is one of LA's most pleasant walking areas. The product of a successful revitalization effort in the late 1980s, it is flanked by upscale shops, movie theaters, and restaurants. Street musicians from around the globe perform flamenco, jazz, and hip hop. On Wednesday and Saturday mornings, the farmers' market attracts large crowds.

Third Street Promenade

3 Santa Monica Pier

MAP A3 ▪ At the end of Colorado Ave ▪ Hippodrome: 310-394-8042, open 11am–5pm daily (until 7pm Fri–Sun) ▪ Pacific Park: 310-260-8744 ▪ Santa Monica Pier Aquarium: 310-393-6149

For a variety of entertainment, visit Santa Monica Pier. California's oldest amusement pier (built in 1908) also marks the western terminus of Route 66. Its oldest attraction is the 1922 Looff Carousel, a historic ride that has made many movie appearances. It is located in Pacific Park, a compact amusement park anchored by a solar-powered Ferris wheel. Tucked beneath the pier, the Santa Monica Pier Aquarium is a small, family-oriented facility where you can observe local marine life.

4 Bergamot Arts Center

MAP C3 ▪ 2525 Michigan Ave, Santa Monica, 310-586-6488 ▪ Opening hours for galleries vary ▪ www.visit bergamot.com

This former historic trolley station has been renovated into a cultural complex housing nearly three dozen galleries, shops, artists' studios, and a café. A highlight is the City Garage Theatre, which plays host to a variety of cutting-edge contemporary productions round the year. Special events and receptions, designed to keep the community involved in creative processes, are frequently organized by other galleries and businesses in the area. Parking here is free.

Bridge over the Venice Canals

5 Venice Canals

MAP B6 ▪ Between Washington & Venice Blvds

Only 3 miles (5 km) remain of Abbot Kinney's original network of canals. The area, which once languished, has become a beautiful, upscale neighborhood. A narrow walkway that is known as the Venice Canal Walk threads through here.

THE "FATHER OF VENICE"

Venice sprang from the vision of tobacco magnate Abbot Kinney (1850–1920), who transformed the soggy marshland lying south of Santa Monica into a canal-laced, oceanfront theme park complete with gondolas and an amusement pier. It opened on July 4 1905, and was a grand success, until fire destroyed most of the theme park facilities in 1920.

6 Venice Boardwalk

MAP A5 ▪ Ocean Front Walk between Venice Blvd & Rose Ave

It is perhaps fitting that Venice Beach, masterminded by an eccentric visionary named Abbot Kinney, is LA's epicenter of counterculture. The circus-like scene reigning along the seaside boardwalk – officially known as "Ocean Front Walk" – must be seen to be believed (see p124). The area is best avoided after dark.

7 Marina del Rey

MAP B6 ▪ South of Venice Beach ▪ Visitors' Bureau ▪ 4701 Admiralty Way ▪ 310-305-9545

With over 6,000 yachts and pleasure boats, Marina del Rey is the largest small-craft harbor in the world and the place to come for those seeking fun on the water. Active types could explore the harbor on kayaks. You can also catch a dinner cruise, book a whale-watching trip (January to March), or charter a sport fishing boat. A favorite landlubber activity is a sunset dinner at one of the many excellent restaurants.

Picturesque Marina del Rey

(8) Wayfarers Chapel

MAP D4 ■ 5755 Palos Verdes Dr South ■ 310-377-7919 ■ Open 9am–5pm

The most famous structure by Frank Lloyd Wright is a striking 1951 glass-and-stone memorial to 18th-century theologian Emanuel Swedenborg. The chapel features landscaped grounds, a reflecting pool and terraced amphitheater.

Glazed nave, Wayfarer's Chapel

(9) Palos Verdes Peninsula

MAP D5 ■ Follow Palos Verdes Dr along the coast ■ Point Vicente Lighthouse: 31501 Palos Verdes Dr West ■ South Coast Botanic Garden: 26300 Crenshaw Blvd

A drive along the coastline here affords great ocean views with Catalina Island (see pp42–3) in the distance. Malaga Cove and Abalone Cove are popular for their tidepools, and Point Vicente is good for whale-watching. Flower lovers should head to the South Coast Botanic Garden.

(10) South Bay

MAP C3

Three picture-perfect beach towns line the southern end of Santa Monica Bay. Of these, Manhattan Beach (see p51) is the most sophisticated, Hermosa (see p51) is the liveliest, and Redondo (see p50) is the most historical. A paved trail parallel to the beach and connecting all the three communities is perfect for bicycling and inline skating.

A DAY AT THE BEACH

▶ MORNING

Start your day with a drive north along the Pacific Coast Highway for glorious ocean views. Travel to sheltered **Paradise Cove** (Pacific Coast Hwy, Malibu) for breakfast at the pleasant beachfront restaurant, followed by a couple of hours of frolicking in the surf here or a few miles north at **Zuma Beach** (see p50).

Head back south, stopping at **Malibu Adamson House** (see p121) to admire beautiful ceramic tiles before walking over to **Surfrider Beach** (see p50) to watch the world's finest surfers in action.

Then it's off to Santa Monica. Stroll beneath the towering palms of the bluff-top **Palisades Park** (see p53) with the ocean at your feet. For better views of city and sea, treat yourself to a ride on the Ferris wheel on **Santa Monica Pier** (see p121) and perhaps a snack from one of the pier's many vendors.

AFTERNOON

For the rest of the afternoon, rent a bicycle and become part of LA's beach scene during the ride south to Venice along the paved beach-front bike trail. Park the bike or push it along the bizarre **Venice Boardwalk** (see p124), perhaps stopping to get a tattoo (henna or ink), visit a fortune teller, stock up on unique souvenirs, or tank up on gourmet sausages from **Jody Maroni's** (see p124). If time permits, continue south to **Marina del Rey**, one of the world's largest yacht harbors, before heading back to Santa Monica for dinner.

See map on pp120–21

Venice Boardwalk Attractions

1 Windward Avenue
Flanking Windward Avenue are Venice's oldest Renaissance-style buildings, including St. Marks Hotel, a hostel.

2 Sidewalk Café
1401 Ocean Front Walk
▪ 310-399-5547
The kitchen produces satisfying sandwiches, salads, and other simple fare. A perfect spot for people-watching.

3 Muscle Beach Venice
Check out beefy, hunky bodybuilders with abs of steel at this outdoor gym, successor to the Santa Monica original, which shut in 1959.

4 Basketball Courts
The game's always on at Venice's famous outdoor courts, especially during "Hoops by the Beach," which draws the best street basketball teams.

5 Street Performers
The best in the business, Boardwalk's street performers dance, walk barefoot on glass, balance people on their chin, and even juggle chainsaws.

6 Venice Pier
Abbott Kinney built Venice's first pier back in 1905, but the current model dates from 1963. Rescued from demolition in the mid-1980s, the restored fishing pier reopened in 1997.

7 Drum Circle
People of all backgrounds and ages gather on the beach on Sunday afternoons, chanting and dancing to the infectious rhythms of pots, bells, and bottles.

8 Beach Architecture
Unique private homes line the Boardwalk between Venice and Washington Boulevards. Look for the one by Steven Ehrlich at No. 2311 and Frank Gehry's eccentric Norton House at No. 2509.

9 Jody Maroni's Sausage Kingdom
2011 Ocean Front Walk
▪ 310-822-5639
The simple sausage goes gourmet at this very popular yet rather unassuming take-out stand.

10 Murals
Venice Reconstituted, 25 Windward Ave at Speedway ▪ Starry Night, Boardwalk at Wavecrest Ave
Numerous murals beautify facades all along the Venice Boardwalk and its side streets. Rip Cronk's *Venice Reconstituted* and *Homage to a Starry Night* are the most famous.

The 700-ft (213-m) Venice Pier

Unique Main Street Boutiques

**1 Angel City Books
& Records**
MAP B4 ■ 218 Pier Ave, just off
Main St ■ 310-399-8767
Bookworms in search of rare and
out-of-print books should look no
further. A great café next door, too.

Products on display at Caro Bambino

2 Caro Bambino
MAP B4 ■ 2710 Main St
■ 310-399-7971
Everything for the new mother is sold
at this family-owned boutique, from
quality natural baby products and
toys to stylish toddler apparel, and
nursery furniture.

3 Muji
MAP B5 ■ 2936 Main St
■ 310-566-8345
This Japanese minimalist retailer
is known for its natural-fiber, non-
label apparel. You'll also find simple
stationery, travel items, dishes and
tableware, as well as furniture and
bedding on its two floors.

4 Heist
MAP B3 ■ 1100 Abbot Kinney
Blvd ■ 310-450-6531
A posh, elegant store with a wide
selection of designer wear, including
riding boots, cozy knits, and slinky
dresses on offer.

5 Arts & Letters
MAP B5 ■ 2665 Main St
■ 310-392-9076
This stationery store stocks hundreds
of artist-made greeting cards, pens,
and guest books. They also create
custom-made invitations.

6 Vital Hemp
MAP B5 ■ 2305 Main St
■ 310-450-2260
Soft, comfortable, and casual
eco-friendly hemp clothing that is
produced locally and guaranteed to
last longer than cotton or bamboo.

7 ZJ Boarding House
MAP B5 ■ 2619 Main St
■ 800-205-7795
This store is for people with a
passion for boards – the surf, skate,
or snow variety. The knowledgeable
staff help to pick through the huge
selection of gear.

8 Bazar
MAP B5 ■ 1108C Abbot Kinney
Blvd ■ 310-314-2101
A staple since 1998, Bazar has a
rotating blend of vintage clothing,
Italian bath products, textiles, furniture,
jewelry and European-style decor.

9 jAdis
MAP B5 ■ 2701 Main St
■ 310-396-3477
A prop- and curiosity shop for sci-fi
filmmakers, with spare-part robots,
electrical gadgets, Zeppelins, and
many other quirky items.

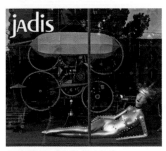
Gadgets in the jAdis window

10 Shoop's Delicatessen
MAP B5 ■ 2400 Main St
■ 310-452-1019
This gourmet deli and café stocks
Continental delicacies but special-
izes in hard-to-find German imports.

See map on pp120–21

Outdoor Pursuits

1 Hiking
Around 600 miles (970 km) of hiking trails meander through the Santa Monica Mountains, stretching from Griffith Park in Hollywood to the north of Malibu. Will Rogers State Park and Topanga State Park are good gateways for hiking.

2 Inline Skating
Enjoy this 22-mile (35-km) paved trail parallel to the beach from Temescal Canyon Road north of Santa Monica to Torrance Beach. Rental outfitters are abundant.

3 Sailing
Marina Boat Rentals: Fisherman's Village, Marina del Rey, 310-574-2822
Skipper around the marina or cruise out to the open ocean with your very own sailboat. Rental outfits usually have a variety for you to choose from.

4 Boogie Boarding
Enjoy the thrill of the waves on a boogie board – it's easy and fun. All the towns on the beach have rental stations on or near the sand.

5 Bicycling
The paved beach path is equally popular for slow bike cruises. Mountain bikers have plenty to explore in the Santa Monica Mountains.

Bicycling on Venice Boardwalk

6 Kayaking
One of the nicest places for sea kayaking is off the coast of Catalina Island (see pp42–3). Traveling leisurely by yourself allows you to explore its craggy coastline and to discover your own secret cove.

Surfing off Surfrider Beach

7 Surfing
The archetypal California watersport is practiced all along the coast – Surfrider Beach (see p50) in Malibu is most famous, but Manhattan Beach (see p51) and Palos Verdes (see p123) are equally popular.

8 Hang-Gliding
Windsports: 818-367-2430, www.windsports.com
Learn to take to the skies while training on beachside "bunny" hills or launch from a height of 3,500 ft (1,070 m) on a breathtaking flight.

9 Windsurfing
Captain Kirk's (for gear rental & lessons): 310-833-3397
Cabrillo Beach (see p51), nicknamed "Hurricane Gulch," is LA's windsurfing mecca. The harbor side is good for beginners, while advanced surfers can make for the open ocean.

10 Fishing
It is permitted to fish without a license off any ocean pier. Sport fishing boats leave from Fisherman's Village in Marina del Rey (see p122), Shoreline Village in Long Beach, and Ports O' Call Village in San Pedro.

Places to Eat

PRICE CATEGORIES
Price categories include a three-course meal for one, a glass of house wine, and all unavoidable extra charges including tax.

$ under $25 $$ $25–$50 $$$ $50–$80
$$$$ over $80

1 Inn of the Seventh Ray
MAP B2 ■ 128 Old Topanga Canyon Rd, off Pacific Coast Hwy ■ 310-455-1311 ■ $$

Tucked away in leafy Topanga Canyon, this creekside retreat offers organic vegetarian, fish, and chicken dishes seasoned with a generous sprinkling of New Age philosophy.

2 Father's Office
MAP C2 ■ 1018 Montana Ave, Santa Monica ■ 310-393-2337 ■ $

This old neighborhood bar has good microbrews and tapas, although regulars swear by the gourmet burger. Delicious fries.

3 Valentino
MAP C2 ■ 3115 Pico Blvd, Santa Monica ■ 310-829-4313 ■ $$$

A wine cellar with around 150,000 curated Italian wines and a menu of fresh Italian cuisine makes Valentino's a favorite. Ask for the "extravaganza", a selection of the best.

4 Michael's
MAP B3 ■ 1147 3rd St, Santa Monica ■ 310-451-0843 ■ $$$$

The romantic garden is a luscious setting for Oscar-worthy Californian cuisine and spot-on service.

5 Chinois on Main
MAP B4 ■ 2709 Main St, Santa Monica ■ 310-392-9025 ■ $$$

A Franco-Chinese menu includes Cantonese duck in plum sauce. Jacket and tie required.

6 Tender Greens
MAP B3 ■ 201 Arizona Ave ■ 310-587-2777 ■ $

Healthy, fresh food sourced from local farmers is the emphasis at this growing chain. Order at the counter and take a seat. Favorites include the albacore sandwich, the kale salad, and the falafel wrap.

7 Fritto Misto
MAP A4 ■ 601 Colorado Blvd ■ 310-458-2829 ■ $$

Come hungry to this friendly Italian café. Pasta-lovers will delight at the "create your own pasta" option. Choose a pasta, a sauce, and some add ins and expect perfection.

8 Border Grill
MAP B3 ■ 1445 4th St, Santa Monica ■ 310-451-1655 ■ $$

Chefs Mary Sue Milliken and Susan Feniger serve up their unique blend of Mexican flavors. Try the delicious rock shrimp ceviche.

Colorful Mexican decor, Border Grill

9 Mélisse
MAP B3 ■ 1104 Wilshire Blvd, Santa Monica ■ 310-395-0881 ■ $$$$

This two-Michelin-starred dining spot uses fresh local ingredients and offers classic French cuisine with a modern twist.

10 Chez Melange
MAP D4 ■ 1716 S Pacific Coast Highway, Redondo Beach ■ 310-540-1222 ■ $$

The menu offers a United Nations of dishes, from sushi to schnitzel.

See map on pp120–21

🔟 Coastal Orange County

Rent a convertible, put the top down, and turn the radio up. Pacific Coast Highway (or PCH as the locals call it) runs 42 miles (68 km) alongside sweeping stretches of beach with vast ocean views and secluded coves with tide pools bursting with marine life. Come here to have fun and experience the sun-drenched coastal lifestyle. Sometimes called the "California Riviera" for its palatial five-star hotels, multimillion dollar homes, and yacht harbors, Orange County (OC) also has charming cottages, gardens, and communities that haven't changed much in the last 50 years. You can walk on piers, ride an old-fashioned Ferris wheel, admire surfers, stroll through art galleries, splash in the water, watch passersby from sidewalk cafés, or simply gaze out over the ocean.

Seafront properties in the beach town of San Clemente

COASTAL ORANGE COUNTY

- **1** Top 10 Sights
  see pp129–31
- **①** Places to Eat
  see p133
- **①** Art Experiences
  in Laguna Beach
  see p132

① San Clemente

Center stage in the late 1960s and early 1970s as the location of "the Western White House" during the Nixon presidency, San Clemente still has the feeling of a normal, non-touristy California beach town. Downtown is filled with affordable restaurants and cafés, as well as antiques, apparel, and gift shops. The town's main attraction, though, is its clean sandy beach and pier. At the far south end of town, surfers rate the Trestles spots as some of the best on this stretch of coast.

② Bolsa Chica Ecological Reserve

MAP F5 ■ Huntington Beach ■ www.bolsachica.org

A world away from the coastal beach culture, this preserve is a wonderful place to walk. An easy 1.5-mile (2.4-km) trail loops through 2 sq miles (5 sq km) of restored salt marsh (one of Southern California's largest), lowlands, and mesa, which are home to 200 species of migratory birds. Displays point out the varieties of herons, egrets, plovers, terns, and ospreys that roost here, as well as the mussels, clams, and 50 species of fish present.

③ Huntington Beach

Known as "Surf City USA" in no small part because of the consistent waves that break along 8 miles (13 km) of uninterrupted sand beach, Huntington Beach is home to the world's largest surfing

Surfing off Huntington Beach

competition and to the International Surfing Museum. Generally, it's a young crowd that comes here to hit the beach and surf during the day, and to enjoy a meal and a drink at night. Huntington has traditionally been far more affordable than other beach towns further down the coast.

Tide pools, Crystal Cove State Park

④ Crystal Cove State Park

MAP G6 ■ 8471 Pacific Coast Highway, Laguna Beach ■ www.crystalcovestatepark.org

Over 3 miles (5 km) of unspoiled shoreline, tide pools, and secluded coves are yours to explore here. Offshore, you may see a pod of dolphins frolicking by or even a few California gray whales. Along part of the beach, 46 vintage cottages (many of which you can rent) make up the Crystal Cove Historic District, which exemplifies early 20th-century coastal living. Across the Pacific Coast Highway, numerous back-country trails are open to hikers and mountain bikers.

⑤ Seal Beach

Head to this low-key ocean playground just south of the San Gabriel River for a taste of small-town America. On tree-lined Main Street you'll find cafés and restaurants. Don't miss walking out on Seal Beach's classic 1,865-ft (570-m) wooden fishing pier. Warm waters and small to mid-size waves make it ideal for swimmers and surfers, while kite surfers flock here for the consistent breeze.

THAT WORTHLESS COASTAL LAND

From 1784 to 1846, the governments of Spain and Mexico awarded vast tracts of land in reward for military service and to encourage settlement. Most of Orange County belonged to this "rancho" system except for Laguna Beach, its rocky coastline deemed unusable. Nowadays, ocean-front properties in that useless coastal land **(below)** are selling for $30 million.

6 Balboa Island

This coveted piece of OC real estate holds one of the most charming villages of Newport Beach. Cottages are densely packed on narrow streets bearing the name of precious stones. The residents of Balboa Island form a small community and relish their laid-back lifestyle. Restaurants, galleries, and boutiques line either side of Marine Avenue, Balboa Island's main shopping street.

7 Laguna Beach

Maybe it's for the light – so similar to that of the south of France – or the romantic secluded coves or the way the hillsides tumble down to the sea, where waves break over the rocks, that artists have been drawn to the spectacular setting that is Laguna Beach for over 100 years. It is still very much an art town, although skyrocketing real-estate prices have recently changed the town's character. You'll still find quaint cottages with flower-filled gardens on side streets, charming arcades with tiny shops, and a gorgeous coastline.

8 Dana Point

MAP G6 ■ Captain Dave's Dolphin Safari: www.dolphin safari.com

Richard Henry Dana wrote in his epic 19th-century book *Two Years Before the Mast* that this area was one the most beautiful spots on this stretch of coast. Today, Dana Point has a vague New England look in homage to its namesake and a harbor busy with activities, including kayaking, paddle boarding, and tide pooling. Because of its unique offshore geology, the ocean here boasts one of the world's richest marine mammal environments. Don't miss a trip on Captain Dave's Dolphin Safari, a catamaran excursion taking you up close to whales and dolphins.

9 Mission San Juan Capistrano

MAP H6 ■ 26801 Ortega Hwy, San Juan Capistrano ■ www.missions jc.com

The seventh in a chain of 21 Spanish missions, this was known as the "Jewel of the Missions." Founded in 1776 by Father (now Saint) Junípero Serra, the Serra Chapel is the state's oldest building. Especially noteworthy

Mission San Juan Capistrano

is its 400-year-old Spanish *retablo*, a fine Baroque altar of handcarved wood overlaid with gold leaf. The mission gardens are lovely places to linger, while exhibitions in surrounding galleries explore aspects of early California life. Every March 19, the return of the swallows from Argentina launches a fiesta celebration in the mission and town.

⑩ Newport Beach

Few towns can outdo Newport Beach for making a grandiose first impression. Mega-yachts tie up side by side in its harbor; Rolls-Royce dealerships line the Coast Highway, and mansions perch on the hillsides. Spread out along the coast and into the hills, Newport Beach consists of several distinct areas, such as the down-to-earth Balboa Peninsula with a boardwalk that's popular with walkers and cyclists, and European-style Corona del Mar filled with trendy shops and upscale eateries.

The scenic Newport Beach

A DAY IN BALBOA

▶ MORNING

Begin your day on the bridge leading over to **Balboa Island**. Stroll down **Marine Avenue** checking out the boutiques and cafés. A dedicated pedestrian sidewalk wends its way around the entire circumference of the island. To your left is the harbor filled with sailboats, yachts, and canopied electric boats. To your right the sidewalk is lined with delightful cottages and gardens. After half a mile (1 km) is the **Balboa Island Ferry** *(410 S Bay Front, Newport Beach)*. Operating since 1919, the ferry carries three cars, bicyclists, and pedestrians across the harbor to the Balboa Peninsula. Ride the ferry to the **Newport Fun Zone**. Take a ride on the Ferris Wheel for a great view of the harbor. At the Fun Zone Boat Company, one 45-minute harbor tour passes by the yachts and mansions and another goes out to the harbor entrance, where you'll see sea lions. A good lunch option is **Ruby's Diner** *(949-675-7829)* at the end of 1 Balboa Pier.

AFTERNOON

After lunch, rent a beach cruiser bicycle and ride along the 3-mile (5-km) long boardwalk between two piers on the beach side of the Peninsula. Spend your afternoon enjoying the friendly beach town. At the end of the day back on Marine Avenue, reward yourself with a chocolate-covered frozen banana from one of the shops on the right-hand side of the street. They've been making them there since 1945.

See map on p128 ←

Art Experiences in Laguna Beach

1 Festival of Arts and Pageant of the Masters

MAP G6 ■ 650 Laguna Canyon Rd ■ 949-494-1145 ■ Jul–Aug ■ www.foapom.com

This festival showcases the art of over 140 local artists. In an amphitheater, live models, elaborate sets, and an orchestra re-create famous paintings.

Sawdust Art Festival stall

2 Sawdust Art Festival

MAP G6 ■ 935 Laguna Canyon Rd ■ 949-494-3030 ■ Jun–Aug ■ www.sawdustartfestival.org

Laguna Beach artists exhibit original handmade crafts, and there are artist demonstrations and live music.

3 Laguna College of Art and Design Gallery

MAP G6 ■ 374 Ocean Ave ■ 949-376-6000 ■ Tours: by appt only ■ www.lcad.edu

Students from this highly regarded art college display their works in a downtown gallery open to the public.

4 Laguna Art Museum

MAP G6 ■ 307 Cliff Dr ■ 949-494-8971 ■ Open 11am–5pm Fri–Tue (until 9pm Thu) ■ Adm ■ www.lagunaartmuseum.org

The focus is on Californian art, with a vast collection of works from the early 19th century to the present.

5 First Thursdays Art Walk

www.firstthursdaysartwalk.com

On the first Thursday of every month, galleries hold demonstrations, receptions, and, often, live music.

6 Public Art

Over 65 pieces of public art are on display throughout town. Be on the lookout in Heisler Park, the Coast Highway, or downtown.

7 Dawson Cole Fine Art

MAP G6 ■ 326 Glenneyre St ■ 888-972-5543 ■ Open 10am–6pm Mon–Sat, 11am–6pm Sun ■ www.dawsoncolefineart.com

Come here to view the exquisite bronze sculptures of contemporary figurative artist Richard MacDonald. Don't miss the sculpture garden.

8 Redfern Gallery

MAP G6 ■ 1540 S Coast Hwy ■ 949-497-3356 ■ Open 11am–5pm daily ■ www.redferngallery.com

American Impressionists with an emphasis on early California *plein air* artists, such as William Wendt and Edgar Payne, are exhibited here.

9 Wyland Gallery

MAP G6 ■ 509 S Coast Hwy ■ 949-376-8000 ■ Open 9am–9pm daily ■ www.wyland.com

Marine artist Robert Wyland painted his first of 100 outdoor whaling walls just next door. On sale are original paintings, prints, and sculptures.

10 John Barber Glass Designs

MAP G6 ■ 21062 Laguna Cyn Rd ■ 949-494-1464 ■ Check opening hours ■ johnbarberglassdesigns.com

Tucked in a wooded area of Laguna Canyon, the studio and showroom of this master glass blower is a fantastic glimpse into an artist's world. Pieces are quite affordable.

Places to Eat

1 25 Degrees
MAP F5 ▪ 412 Walnut Ave, Huntington Beach ▪ 714-960-2525 ▪ $$

High-end gourmet burgers are fashioned to your desire. Choose from ground sirloin, tuna, turkey, or veggie and go from there. Garlic fries are a must, as is a spiked milkshake.

2 The Beachcomber Cafe
MAP G6 ▪ 15 Crystal Cove, Newport Coast ▪ 949-376-6900 ▪ $$

Soak in the ocean view with coconut macadamia pancakes for breakfast or watch the sunset with lobster pasta at this prime-location café.

3 Mastro's Ocean Club
MAP F5 ▪ 8112 East Coast Hwy, Newport Beach ▪ 949-376-6990 ▪ $$$

Romantic and sophisticated, Maestro offers steak and seafood cooked to perfection. Start with a seafood tower made to order and finish with their famous warm butter cake.

4 Zinc Café
MAP G6 ▪ 350 Ocean Ave, Laguna Beach ▪ 949-494-6302 ▪ $$

Claim a table in the outdoor patio and order your food at the counter at this popular café. Vegetarians will love the choices – everything from potato enchiladas to avocado toast.

5 Las Brisas
MAP G6 ▪ 361 Cliff Dr, Laguna Beach ▪ 949-497-5434 ▪ $$

Mexican seafood with a California twist is the main feature here, along with its breathtaking coastal

The patio at Las Brisas

PRICE CATEGORIES
Price categories include a three-course meal for one, a glass of house wine, and all unavoidable extra charges including tax.

$ under $25 $$ $25–$50 $$$ $50–$80 $$$$ over $80

views – you can't go wrong for breakfast, lunch, or dinner. The patio is the place for margaritas.

6 Splashes
MAP G6 ▪ 1555 S Coast Hwy, Laguna Beach ▪ 877-741-5908 ▪ $$$$

Situated just off the beach at the Surf & Sand Hotel, Splashes is elegant yet casual and very romantic. Breakfasts are excellent but pricey

7 Mozambique
MAP G6 ▪ 1740 S Coast Hwy ▪ 949-715-7777 ▪ $$$

Gorgeous dining rooms provide the ambience for excellent Southern African dishes. The rooftop hosts the best happy hour in Laguna Beach.

8 La Sirena Grill
MAP G6 ▪ 30862 S Coast Hwy, Laguna Beach ▪ 949-499-2301 ▪ $

A favorite with locals, this is the place for fresh, well-prepared Mexican food. Calamari tacos are excellent, as are the veggie enchiladas. Twenty craft beers are on tap.

9 Ramos House Café
MAP H6 ▪ 31752 Los Rios St, San Juan Capistrano ▪ 949-443-1342 ▪ $$

In a 19th-century home in the Rios District, the Ramos House serves a delicious brunch. The smoked bacon scramble and apple cinnamon beignets are especially tasty.

10 The Fisherman's Restaurant & Bar
MAP H7 ▪ 611 Avenida Victoria, San Clemente ▪ 949-498-6390 ▪ $$

Situated at the base of the town pier, the most coveted tables overlook the ocean. Enjoy seafood while watching the surfers with the sunset beyond.

See map on p128

Streetsmart

Mural behind the Hollywood Wax
Museum, Hollywood Boulevard

Getting To and
  Around Los Angeles   **136**

Practical Information   **138**

Places to Stay   **144**

General Index   **152**

Acknowledgments   **159**

Getting To and Around Los Angeles

Arriving by Air

Three main airports serve the region: **Los Angeles International (LAX)**, Burbank's **Bob Hope Airport**, and Santa Ana/Orange County's **John Wayne Airport**.

Nearly 75 airlines serve LAX, making it one of the world's busiest airports.

Compared to using other major world airports, arriving at LAX and leaving the airport can be confusing. When exiting baggage claim, color-coded signs indicate where you need to wait depending on where you are going and by what mode of transport. Rental cars, shuttles, shared ride vans, buses, taxis as well as hotels, have differently-colored signs.

Blue signs indicate the LAX bus connection, with Bus A continuously circling the terminals, Bus C going to Parking Lot C and the city bus terminal, and Bus G to the Metro Rail Green Line at Aviation/LAX station.

Green signs indicate the Flyaway Buses, with service to Union Station, Santa Monica, and Hollywood (credit card only), as well as hourly buses for the Disney Resort and hotels.

Near the Pasadena area, Bob Hope Airport is served by seven airlines in two terminals. Metrolink and Amtrak stop across the street at a small station.

John Wayne Airport has limited international flights from Vancouver, Canada, and a few cities in Mexico. The **Disney Resort Bus** leaves from here every hour.

Arriving by Train

Amtrak trains arriving at the historic Union Station in Downtown include the Coast Starlight from Seattle, the Southwest Chief from Chicago, and the Sunset Limited from Orlando. The Pacific Surfliner service from San Diego to Santa Barbara also stops here.

Arriving by Bus

Greyhound operates a huge network of air-conditioned coaches all across the US. Bus travel is inexpensive but slow and is a suitable option only if you're arriving from nearby cities such as San Francisco or Las Vegas. Buses stop at the main Greyhound terminal in an industrial section of Downtown, an area best avoided after dark. **Megabus** connects with San Francisco, stopping at Union Station.

Arriving by Car

Several freeways lead straight to and through LA, including the I-5, Hwy 101, and I-405 from the north; the I-10 from the east; and the I-5 and I-405 from the south. Try to time your arrival in LA to avoid the morning rush-hour traffic from 6:30am to 9am.

Traveling by Train

Amtrak's Pacific Surfliner travels from Los Angeles to Anaheim. **Metrolink**, a regional commuter rail system also connects LA to Anaheim and stops further south in Orange County. Another useful line goes from Union Station to Burbank and the San Fernando Valley. Metrolink trains operate from the early morning into the evening.

Traveling by Light Rail and Subway

MTA operates six rail lines on **LA Metro Rail** – the Red Line, the city's only subway route, goes from Union Station to Universal City. The Purple Line parallels this as far as Wilshire/Vermont. The Gold Line also goes from Union Station to Pasadena and beyond. The Blue Line travels from 7th Street/Metro Center station to Long Beach, and the Expo Line runs to Culver City with an extension continuing to Santa Monica. The Green Line crosses LA from Norwalk to El Segundo (Aviation Station for LAX), and Redondo Beach.

If you are planning to take public transportation for more than a few rides, consider buying a **TAP Card** in any Metro Rail station or from vendors in popular tourist areas. You can store value or add a 1-, 7-, or 30-day pass to the card (use any stored value before loading a pass). TAP Cards are good on all public transport in LA County.

Traveling by Bus

The MTA bus network covers just about anywhere you want to go in LA, if you have the time. For visitors, the most useful routes are those running from Downtown to Santa Monica, Beverly Hills, and Hollywood.

Standard one-ride bus fares are $1.75 with no transfers, cash only.

Santa Monica operates its own bus network, the **Big Blue Bus**. Especially useful routes for visitors are the Rapid #10, between Santa Monica and Downtown, the #3, from Santa Monica to the LAX area, and the #1 between Santa Monica and Venice Beach.

DASH buses provide a frequent service to Union Station, Chinatown, Little Tokyo, the Fashion District, LA Live, and the Music Center.

Traveling by Car

A car is still the best way to get around. Distances are vast and freeways are challenging. Always allow plenty of time, especially during the morning and evening rush hours when gridlock is common.

Study all parking restriction signs, including what's posted on the meter as you'll often find information in different spots. Parking enforcement is aggressive. Right-hand turns are permitted at red lights unless otherwise posted.

All popular car-rental agencies are represented in the area.

Traveling by Taxi

Getting around town by taxi can be a pricey proposition unless you're traveling as a group or are only going a short distance. Taxi drivers usually won't respond to being hailed but must be ordered in advance, from **Checker Cab** or **Yellow Cab**. The Uber app and other ride-sharing services are also options.

Traveling by Bicycle

The good news is LA is mostly flat, while the bad news is you're competing for road space with lots of cars. LA has nearly 600 miles (965 km) of bikeways, which is increasing with the growing popularity of biking. To get across LA on a bike isn't practical, but along the coast from Santa Monica to Redondo Beach, and from Long Beach to Newport Beach in Orange County, it is a delightful means of transportation.

Bicycles can be taken on Metro Rail and Metrolink. Buses in Santa Monica are equipped with front racks for passengers to carry bicycles. Cyclists under age 18 must wear a helmet by law.

Traveling on Foot

With parking at a huge premium, some LA areas are best seen on foot. Leave the car behind and take a stroll in Beverly Hills, Santa Monica, Hollywood, Downtown, Venice, and Pasadena. Pedestrians have the right of way at crossings.

DIRECTORY

ARRIVING BY AIR

Bob Hope Airport
🌐 bobhopeairport.com

Disney Resort Bus
🌐 graylineanaheim.com/airport_info.cfm

John Wayne Airport
🌐 ocair.com

Los Angeles International (LAX)
🌐 lawa.org

ARRIVING BY TRAIN

Amtrak
🌐 amtrak.com

ARRIVING BY BUS

Greyhound
1716 E 7th St
🌐 greyhound.com

Megabus
🌐 us.megabus.com

TRAVELING BY TRAIN

Metrolink
🌐 metrolinktrains.com

TRAVELING BY LIGHT RAIL AND SUBWAY

LA Metro Rail
🌐 metro.net

TAP Card
🌐 taptogo.net

TRAVELING BY BUS

Big Blue Bus
🌐 bigbluebus.com

DASH
🌐 ladottransit.com/dash

TRAVELING BY TAXI

Checker Cab
☎ 800-300-5007

Yellow Cab
☎ 800-200-1085

Practical Information

Passports and Visas

All visitors to the US must have a valid passport. Citizens of 38 countries may enter visa free under the Visa Waver Program for stays of up to 90 days. To use this program you must have an e-Passport embedded with an electronic chip and apply for eligibility through ESTA (Electronic System for Travel Authorization) prior to travel. Everyone else needs a visa. Upon arrival in the US, a Customs and Border Protection Officer will make the final call to allow entry. Be prepared to show a return ticket.

Consulates within the US, including those of the **UK**, **Australia**, **New Zealand**, and **Canada**, are unable to intervene in legal matters, but can provide help and advice to visiting nationals.

Customs Regulations and Immigration

Clearing customs and immigration at LAX can be a lengthy procedure. Even transit passengers must be processed, so lines can be long. There are staff on hand to direct you to the appropriate line. Automated kiosks that scan your passport and scan your picture will issue you a slip of paper that you need to take to an immigration officer.

Everyone over the age of 21 is allowed a liter of liquor and 200 cigarettes duty free. US citizens may bring in $400 worth of gifts and non-US citizens only $100. Cash over the value of $10,000 needs to be declared. Fresh meat, plants, and products from any endangered species are prohibited.

Travel Safety Advice

Visitors can get up-to-date travel safety information from the **UK Foreign and Commonwealth Office**, the **US Department of State**, and the **Australian Department of Foreign Affairs and Trade**.

Travel Insurance

Ensure that you get comprehensive travel insurance before traveling either to or around the US. Double check that this covers you for all eventualities, such as trip interruptions, lost baggage, cancelled or delayed flights and medical expenses.

If you are travelling to the US from abroad, always check with your primary healthcare insurer or provider at home to see if you will be covered while away. The American health care system can be extremely expensive for those without insurance, so while you won't be denied medical care in an emergency room, you can expect to leave with a large bill.

If you are renting a car, establish what your auto insurer and credit card company cover in case of accident or theft. Also check if there are extra payments to be made when the car is returned

Health

No vaccinations are required for visitors entering the US.

Don't underestimate the effects of overdoing it in hot, muggy weather. It's easy to feel exhausted after a day of intensive activity such as hiking (see p126). Although air quality has improved dramatically, sensitive lungs can feel air pollution on certain days, especially the further inland you are.

Enjoy the brilliant sunshine, but slather on the sunscreen during the day and be sure to take a hat whenever you are outdoors. California has one of the country's highest incidences of skin cancer, which is no surprise since most people pursue outdoor activities all year round.

Ocean waters are generally clean, except for three days after a heavy storm. Accumulated and untreated runoff from miles away washes down storm drains and empties into the ocean, and sewer leaks are common. If you go swimming at these times, you can expect to fall sick.

Dangerous riptides can occur along the coast; ask the lifeguards about swimming conditions at the beach. Posted green flags indicate safe swimming, yellow mean caution, and red flags denote hazardous surf. If you are caught in a riptide, let the current carry you down the coast until it dies out, and then swim in to shore.

LA tap water is heavily chlorinated and therefore not particularly tasty, despite being perfectly drinkable. Bottled water is widely available. Free water served in restaurants is always tap water.

Smoking is illegal in most public places, including airports, post offices, stores and theaters, as well as in all restaurants and cafés. Some bars and nightclubs have separate outdoor areas for smoking.

Major drugstores such as CVS, Longs Drugs, and Rite Aid have full-service pharmacies, most of which keep late hours (some are open 24 hours a day). If you take prescription drugs, it's best to bring your own supply.

Personal Security

Despite a reputation to the contrary, Los Angeles is a fairly safe city, especially in touristy neighborhoods. Of course, common sense applies. Be aware of your surroundings when using the ATM and watch your belongings in crowded areas like Venice Beach or Hollywood Boulevard. Having personal property stolen is the most likely crime you may encounter in LA. Never leave items visible in your car.

If you have lost something on a Metro Bus or Rail, allow about three days for your property to be logged into the **Lost and Found** system.

After dark, take care in Venice Beach and some areas of Downtown and Hollywood. Walk away from problems before they escalate, especially when leaving bars and nightclubs. If approached, a polite "sorry, not today" is usually enough to be left alone.

LA is a cosmopolitan city, and women travelers should not have any special problems. Gaining admission to trendy nightclubs is much easier for women than for men. It is always wise to be alert to your surroundings, especially after dark. Do not walk on the beach alone at night and be careful in parking lots. Take the usual precautions at hotels and be aware of your surroundings.

Emergency Services

Dial 911 for **ambulance**, **fire**, or **police**. This toll-free number will be answered by an operator, who will send out the respective emergency response service. In a serious emergency, medical assistance is available 24 hours a day in hospital emergency rooms. Cheaper options can be urgent care clinics, which accept patients on a walk-in basis. Expect to pay for services before treatment. Call your insurance company for a referral to a local doctor.

Travelers with Specific Needs

Los Angeles is a relatively accessible place for those with visual, mobility, or hearing impairments. By law, all public buildings, museums, and restaurants must have wheelchair access. Sidewalk curbs are cut to facilitate movement, hotels have rooms with extra wide doors, and car-rental agencies offer special hand-controlled cars. Buses are equipped with wheelchair lifts and all LA Metro Rail stations are wheelchair accessible.

DIRECTORY

PASSPORTS AND VISAS

Australia
2029 Century Park East, Ste. 3150
310-229-2300

Canada
550 South Hope St, 9th floor
213-346-2700

New Zealand
2425 Olympic Blvd, Ste. 600E, Santa Monica
310-566-6555

UK
2029 Century Park East, Ste. 1350
310-789-0031

TRAVEL SAFETY ADVICE

Australian Department of Foreign Affairs and Trade
dfat.gov.au
smartraveller.gov.au

UK Foreign and Commonwealth Office
gov.uk/foreign-travel-advice

US Department of State
travel.state.gov

PERSONAL SECURITY

Lost and Found
3571 Pasadena Ave
323-937-8920
lostandfound.metro.net

EMERGENCY SERVICES

Ambulance, Fire, Police
911

Currency and Banking

Paper notes come in denominations of $1, $2, $5, $10, $20, $50, and $100. Rare but still in circulation are $500, $1,000, $5,000, $10,000 and $100,000. Coins are 1¢, 5¢, 10¢, 25¢, 50¢, and $1. There is a slight gold cast to some $1 coins and they are slightly larger and heavier than a 25¢ coin. If paying for anything in cash with a merchant, expect to have any paper bills larger than a $20 scrutinized. Quarters are useful for parking meters, buses, laundromats, and vending machines.

LAX has international exchange kiosks, but rates are not competitive. **LA Currency** offers good rates and has locations in Downtown and in Hollywood. Major banks handle most transactions, but bring at least two forms of ID. Large hotels often exchange currency as well, but often offer bad rates.

There are 24-hour ATMs (Automatic Teller Machines) all over the city. Look behind your ATM or credit card to see which banking network it's associated with. ATMs inside convenience stores or malls charge you for the privilege, as can your own bank if you go outside the network.

Most major banks are found throughout Los Angeles. Banking hours are usually from 9 or 10am to 6pm Monday to Friday, with Saturday hours from 9am to 1 or 2pm.

Visa and MasterCard credit and debit cards are widely accepted, Diners Club and American Express cards slightly less so, especially in smaller shops. If you are using a non-US issued credit card, make sure the card has a magnetic strip on the back, as chip-and-pin readers are not always in use. Travelers' checks are quite hard to cash.

Telephone and Internet

Coin telephones are hard to find in Los Angeles, but they still exist at LAX, some transit areas, hospitals, some hotels and restaurants, and government buildings. You can contact emergency services at 911 without coins from any of these phones. Disposable cell phones with pre-set calling amounts are readily available at most convenience stores.

If you carry an unlocked phone, you can find SIM cards to fit it with a variety of prepaid, no-contract plans at supermarkets and corner stores. T-Mobile and AT&T stores also carry SIM cards. If your home is outside the country, the best way to communicate is through Wi-Fi, using Skype or the phone app WhatsApp. Free Wi-Fi hotspots are everywhere: cafés, fast-food restaurants, shopping centers, and bookstores are common spots to find them. Public libraries usually also have computer terminals to use, as do hostels, but you must be a guest. Most hotels offer free Wi-Fi, as does LAX. High-end hotels usually charge for Internet access.

Postal Services

Depending on the branch, postoffice hours are 8:30am to 5pm Monday to Friday, with some branches open on Saturday mornings. Post offices can be found throughout the city.

Stamps are usually available from vending machines in the lobby, and signage indicates the cost of postage for mail sent to domestic and international addresses. Stamps can also be found at many supermarkets and franchised mail service stores, which also provide shipping services. Hotel concierges can post mail for you.

FedEx and **UPS** offer courier services with guaranteed overnight delivery and reliable international service. Many of their franchise offices sell packaging supplies. Much cheaper, the **US Postal Service** offers overnight service in the continental US and two- and three-day service internationally.

Television, Radio, and Newspapers

All major television networks have affiliate stations in LA, and there is no shortage of local news stations with helicopters in the sky to cover the latest police chase or red-carpet movie premiere. Educational TV is served by **PBS SoCal**, **KLCS**, and independent **KCET**. Spanish- and Asian-language TV and radio are widely available.

Every genre of music or political persuasion has a radio station for it. News, traffic reports, and talk radio shows reside on the AM dial. KFI 640AM offers local and syndicated talk shows, while KNX 1070AM broadcasts 24-hour news.

On the FM dial, public and college radio stations host National Public Radio-affiliated KCRW 89.9FM, with its variety of eclectic music, in-depth news reporting, and interest stories; KUSC 91.5FM sponsors classical music; and KKJZ 89.9FM has one of the region's better jazz stations.

Surprising for a world city, the *Los Angeles Times* is its only major newspaper. Cities within Los Angeles County publish their own local papers. The free *LA Weekly* is a good source for what's on. You'll find restaurant reviews, and movie, theater, and music listings. Copies can be found throughout the city.

Opening Hours

Most museums are open from 10am to 5pm. Always check the website or call before making plans, since many close one day out of the week.

Stores usually open at 10am and close between 5 and 6pm. Regular hours at malls are 10am to 9pm Monday to Saturday and 11am to 7pm Sunday.

Department stores sometimes open at 7am for super sales or extend their hours during the holiday season. Malls close only during a few major holidays, such as Christmas and New Years; however, some stores may be open on Thanksgiving (the fourth Thursday in November) and Easter Sunday.

You shouldn't have any trouble finding 24-hour convenience stores, gas stations, drug stores, and supermarkets. A few large supermarkets are open 24 hours as well.

Time Difference

From the first Sunday in November until the second Sunday in March, Los Angeles operates on Pacific Standard Time (PST). For the remaining months the clock moves ahead one hour and becomes Pacific Daylight Time (PDT).

Electrical Appliances

The US uses plugs with two flat blades that sometimes have an additional round grounding pin. While either of these will fit into an American socket, those traveling from abroad will need a plug adaptor to use foreign appliances. It is much easier to buy this before you leave as most adaptors sold in the US are for Americans traveling abroad. However, if you do forget to bring an adaptor, some **Best Buy** stores carry them.

Most modern electronics are designed to work on either the 110 or 220 volt system. In America, the power is set at 110 volts and 220-volt devices will not work efficiently without a power converter or a transformer.

While most hotels provide hair dryers, these, like most small appliances, are inexpensive to buy at discount stores.

Weather

LA has a moderate climate with low humidity and cool evenings, even in summer. Rain is most likely from January to March. Late spring often presents what locals call "May gray" and "June gloom," when low cloud cover never seems to end, but just as easily you can get endless days of sun.

Summer is the busiest time of year, with warm days and cool yet pleasant evenings on the coast. Further inland, the temperatures soar, making any time spent outdoors uncomfortable. Showers during this time of year are incredibly rare.

DIRECTORY

CURRENCY AND BANKING

LA Currency
w lacurrency.com

POSTAL SERVICES

FedEx
w fedex.com

UPS
w ups.com

US Postal Service
w usps.com

TELEVISION, RADIO, AND NEWSPAPERS

KCET
w kcet.org

KLCS
w klcs.org

LA Weekly
w laweekly.com

Los Angeles Times
w latimes.com

PBS SoCal
w pbssocal.org

ELECTRICAL APPLIANCES

Best Buy
w bestbuy.com

Visitor Information

The **LA Tourism and Convention Board** maintains a convenient visitor center in Hollywood, where you can pick up a wealth of information. In addition, there are organisations such as **Santa Monica Convention and Visitors' Bureau**, **Beverly Hills Visitors' Bureau**, and **Pasadena Visitors' Bureau**.

Crowd-sourced review websites are fantastic for helping you choose from the city's plentiful attractions and restaurants. Use these sites with care, though, as reviews can often be unreasonable or even fraudulently written.

Trips and Tours

StarLine Tours has run bus tours in Los Angeles and the surrounding area for decades. Tours on the hop-on, hop-off double-decker buses stop at some of the city's most popular locations and you can even opt for a tour that passes the homes of the stars. On board, recorded audio provides narration about everything that you are seeing. StarLine also offers transportation to the region's plentiful amusement parks.

TMZ Tours specializes in driving by the hotspots of the Sunset Strip, Beverly Hills, Hollywood, and wherever else the TV cameras find celebrities to ambush. A popular feature on TMZ buses is a monitor that plays a clip from the TV show of a site before you arrive.

The unique architecture of LA – especially that of Hollywood, Pasadena, and Downtown – is featured in daily in-depth tours run by **Laura Massino's Architecture Tours**. **LA Conservancy Tours** also offer outstanding walking tours of LA's architectural highlights. Themes include the Broadway Historic Theatre District, Historic Downtown, and Art Deco. Tours depart every Saturday morning.

Esotouric travels through the quirky and secret side of LA, covering themes such as Raymond Chandler's literary noir, or retracing the final steps of LA's greatest murder mystery: the Black Dahlia.

Neon Cruise, put on by the Museum of Neon Art, presents nighttime double-decker bus tours of LA's finest examples of neon signs, marquees, and contemporary art.

For those interested in Hollywood macabre and paranormal, crime scenes, and filming sites of your favorite horror film, **Dearly Departed Tours** will take you there.

Shopping

You can find a mall to explore in almost every region of LA, each featuring an almost identical list of stores. If you're in search of a bargain, the best time to shop is around the public holidays.

Far more interesting are the independent boutiques scattered throughout the city – this is where you'll find unusual, ethnic, and vintage items. Santa Monica's Montana Avenue, Main Street, and 3rd Street Promenade are the best spots.

Abbot Kinney Boulevard and Melrose Avenue will appeal to the super stylish. West 3rd Street between La Cienega and Fairfax is also lined with unique shops.

For rock-bottom prices try Downtown's Fashion District, but be prepared to pick through dizzying amounts of merchandise to find quality.

At the other extreme, any boutique on Rodeo Drive in Beverly Hills will happily dress you like a star for the price of a small house.

Dining

With endless choices, people in LA love to go out to eat. From trendy restaurants presided over by god-like celebrity chefs to food trucks with equally fabulous fare, LA eateries offer just about anything you can desire or imagine.

In the better restaurants menus emphasize what's fresh and seasonal with local sourcing. Don't be shy in asking for the availability of gluten-free, lactose-free, non-GMO, and allergy-free food; everybody does it. Ethnic restaurants are one of LA's greater pleasures, with Latin American food leading the way. Or if you crave anything from Ethiopian to Cambodian cuisine, a restaurant somewhere will serve it.

Always reserve and expect to wait once you arrive. Many restaurants subscribe to an online booking service such as **OpenTable**. Unlike restaurants in other countries, where you have a table for the evening, LA restaurants expect you to vacate the table after a certain amount of time – you may start to feel the pressure after you've finished dessert and coffee.

Regardless of one's views on tipping, servers expect at least 15 percent, while 20 percent is the norm. Large parties will find an 18 percent gratuity added to the check.

All restaurants will welcome children; the trick is to go early, when staff have the time to tend to you. If your kids are adventurous eaters, the ethnic restaurants here are especially accommodating. The best places for family-friendly restaurants are Santa Monica Bay and the Disney Resort areas.

Accommodation

LA is vast and the traffic congestion can be bad, so pick a hotel reasonably near the area that you intend to spend most time in to avoid hours on the road every day. In general, anything close to the ocean will be more expensive than similar accommodations elsewhere. Always factor in the price of parking, which can be $45/night in some luxury hotels.

Bed and breakfasts are becoming more common, but they are usually in buildings of charm and historic interest and tend to be expensive – unlike their counterparts in Europe.

All the usual motel chains are represented, but they may not always be in an inspiring location. Parking and Wi-Fi are usually free though.

For those visiting the Disney Resort for multiple days, it's often more sensible to relocate to a hotel in its vicinity. Located in areas of interest for visitors, such as Hollywood, Santa Monica, and Venice, they offer a friendly atmosphere and good budget tips posted on the bulletin boards. It's a good idea to read the reviews on the hostel booking sites to see what you are likely to get. There are no tent camping facilities within an hour's drive of LA.

Rare is a hotel with a standard year-round posted rate. Factors that determine the cost of your room are the time of year and whether it's the middle of the week or the weekend. Summers and holidays are high season. Generally on a weekend, Downtown hotels may be less expensive. Some hotels near the beach will require a minimum two-night stay.

Hotel occupancy tax is 14 percent, and Santa Monica adds a $2/day city tax. Upscale hotels are known for charging resort fees and Wi-Fi access. If you call the hotel directly and not the central reservation number, you may be able to negotiate some of these fees.

Online booking sites, such as **Booking.com** are useful places to look. **Airbnb** is a popular site for private property rentals, which can be a unique – and cheaper – alternative to hotels and hostels. Always read the online reviews carefully, but remember, these aren't always genuine.

DIRECTORY

VISITOR INFORMATION

Beverly Hills Visitors' Bureau
9400 Santa Monica Blvd
☎ 310-248-1015
w lovebeverlyhills.com

LA Tourism and Convention Board
6801 Hollywood Blvd
☎ 323-467-6412
w discoverlosangeles.com

Pasadena Visitors' Bureau
300 E Green St
☎ 626-795-9311
w visitpasadena.com

Santa Monica Convention and Visitors' Bureau
2427 Main St
☎ 310-393-7593
w santamonica.com

TRIPS AND TOURS

Dearly Departed Tours
w dearlydepartedtours.com

Esotouric
w esotouric.com

LA Conservancy Tours
w laconservancy.org/tours

Laura Massino's Architecture Tours
w architecturetoursla.com

Neon Cruise
w neonmona.org

StarLine Tours
w starlinetours.com

TMZ Tours
w tmz.com/tour

DINING

OpenTable
w opentable.com

ACCOMMODATION

Airbnb
w airbnb.com

Booking.com
w booking.com

Places to Stay

PRICE CATEGORIES
For a standard, double room per night (with breakfast if included), taxes and extra charges.

$ under $150	$$ $150–350	$$$ over $350

Luxury Hotels

Beverly Wilshire
MAP J6 ▪ 9500 Wilshire Blvd ▪ 310-275-5200 ▪ www.fourseasons.com ▪ $$$
Overlooking Rodeo Drive, this dignified 1928 hotel has hosted royalty many times and featured prominently in the 1990 movie *Pretty Woman*. Luxurious extras include chauffeured car service within a radius of 3 miles (5 km).

The Four Seasons
MAP K5 ▪ 300 S Doheny Dr ▪ 310-273-2222 ▪ www.fourseasons.com ▪ $$$
This hotel welcomes its guests with enormous floral arrangements. Its delights include a full-service spa and free limousine rides within a 2-mile (3-km) radius. At the Windows Lounge you may find yourself sipping cocktails next to someone famous. Children under 18 stay free with parents.

Hotel Casa del Mar
MAP A4 ▪ 1910 Ocean Way ▪ 310-581-5533 ▪ www.hotelcasadelmar. com ▪ $$$
An imposing presence overlooking Santa Monica Beach, this 1926 beach club has been restored to its original grandeur. The grand, lavish lobby is juxtaposed by the cozily decorated rooms.

Montage Laguna Beach
MAP G6 ▪ 30801 S Coast Hwy, Laguna Beach ▪ 949-715-6000 ▪ montagehotels.com/ lagunabeach ▪ $$$
Atop a 50-ft (15-m) bluff with sweeping views over the Pacific Ocean, this luxury, Craftsman-style hotel is utterly gorgeous. All guestrooms have ocean views and are equipped with amenities such as deep, marble soaking tubs. Priceless early-California paintings grace the walls. Facilities offered also include a full-service spa and large swimming pool.

Oceana Beach Club Hotel
MAP C2 ▪ 849 Ocean Ave ▪ 310-393-0486 ▪ www.hoteloceana santa monica.com ▪ $$$
One of Santa Monica's prettiest hotels, this has a fun, colorful decor that is reminiscent of the French Riviera. Many of the large suites offer guests views of the ocean.

The Peninsula Beverly Hills
MAP J6 ▪ 9882 S Santa Monica Blvd ▪ 310-551-2888 ▪ www.peninsula. com ▪ $$$
Antiques and artwork grace rooms, suites, and villas, all brimming with high-tech features, including wireless internet access and satellite TV. A personal room valet attends to your every need.

Ritz-Carlton Los Angeles
MAP S6 ▪ 900 W Olympic Blvd ▪ 213-743-8800 ▪ www.ritzcarlton.com ▪ $$$
This sleek, modern highly luxurious hotel is close to the Staples Center, the Microsoft Theater, and top shopping and dining options. It shares a tower with the Marriott at LA LIVE and has a posh rooftop pool and bar on the 26th floor.

Terranea Resort
MAP D4 ▪ 6610 Palos Verdes Dr S ▪ 310-802-7433 ▪ www.terranea. com ▪ $$$
Located on the Palos Verdes Peninsula, with splendid views over the ocean and Catalina Island, this eco-friendly resort has 400 rooms, suites, and bungalows. Guests can while away the time at the luxury spa, with 24 treatment rooms, at the nine-hole golf course, or enjoying the gastronomic treats at the restaurant.

Viceroy L'Ermitage
MAP K5 ▪ 9291 Burton Way ▪ 310-278-3344 ▪ www.viceroyhotelsand resorts.com/beverlyhills ▪ $$$
Discretion is key at this sophisticated Beverly Hills hideaway with the full range of in-room high-tech amenities. Enjoy panoramic views from the rooftop pool

flanked by cabanas for extra privacy. Even pets get the royal treatment.

Waldorf Astoria Beverly Hills

MAP J6 ▪ 9850 Wilshire Blvd ▪ 800-774-1500 ▪ www.waldorfastoria beverlyhills.com ▪ $$$

The 21-story gem with Art Deco architecture is located on the spot of the old Trader Vic's and just a few blocks from Rodeo Drive. Facilities include a chic rooftop pool, a complete business center, Bijan menswear boutique, and La Prarie spa.

Historic Hotels

Chateau Marmont

MAP M3 ▪ 8221 W Sunset Blvd ▪ 323-656-1010 ▪ www.chateaumarmont. com ▪ $$

Famous recluses such as Greta Garbo holed up in this quirky French castle-style hotel, whose policy of discretion still ensures steady celebrity bookings. Revel in Hollywood lore in the cottages, bungalows, and suites.

Crystal Cove Beach Cottages

MAP G6 ▪ Crystal Cove State Park Historic District, 35 Crystal Cove, Newport Coast ▪ 800-444-7275 ▪ www.crystal covebeach cottages.org ▪ $$

Step back in time to a quintessential California beach settlement. On the National Register of Historic Places, these 29 adorable self-catering cottages have been painstakingly restored and furnished to retain the lifestyle charm of the period between 1935 and 1955.

No TVs, phones, Wi-Fi, or air-conditioning; just the sounds of the surf to lull you to sleep.

The Georgian Hotel

MAP A3 ▪ 1415 Ocean Ave ▪ 310-395-9945 ▪ www.georgianhotel. com ▪ $$

This 1933 seaside hotel was an instant hit with the movie elite seeking to escape the Hollywood heat. Behind the Art Deco facade await guest rooms in chocolate colors, most with ocean views.

The Hollywood Roosevelt

MAP P2 ▪ 7000 Hollywood Blvd ▪ 323-466-7000 ▪ www.theholly wood roosevelt.com ▪ $$

A stone's throw away from Hollywood & Highland is this famous Hollywood hotel. While the grand lobby pays homage to the original Spanish-Mediterranean decor, most rooms have 21st-century amenities. Only the poolside cabanas retain old-fashioned flair.

Hotel Queen Mary

MAP E4 ▪ 1126 Queens Hwy ▪ 562-435-3511 ▪ www.queenmary.com ▪ $$

Stay in the roomy quarters of the *Queen Mary* ocean liner (see p73). With their wood paneling, Art Deco design and thick carpets to savor the ambience of a bygone era.

The Langham Huntington

MAP E2 ▪ 1401 S Oak Knoll Ave ▪ 626-568-3900 ▪ www.pasadena.lang hamhotels.com ▪ $$

This hotel is a stunning destination in itself. Take

your breakfast alfresco before lounging by the Olympic-sized, heated pool, followed by a session in the full-service spa. Enjoy afternoon high tea in the lobby lounge, then hit the tennis courts before changing for dinner at the steakhouse or at the terrace bistro – a perfect day, indeed.

Millennium Biltmore Hotel Los Angeles

MAP U5 ▪ 506 S Grand ▪ 213-624-1011 ▪ www. millenniumhotels.com ▪ $$

A Downtown architectural landmark, the Biltmore was LA's first luxury hotel when it opened in 1923. It has hosted presidents, celebrities, and even The Beatles, who had to land their helicopter on the rooftop to avoid the fans. It is the site of several Academy Awards ceremonies, as well as a popular film location. This Beaux-Arts hotel has opulent interiors that resemble a Spanish palace. The guest rooms are comfortable.

Shangri-La Hotel

MAP A3 ▪ 1301 Ocean Ave ▪ 310-394-2791 ▪ www.shangrila-hotel. com ▪ $$

Dating from 1939, this boutique hotel has a modern feel. It boasts a landscaped and heated outdoor pool, a relaxing spa as well as a 24-hour fitness center. Its oceanfront Santa Monica location is one of its best features and many of the large rooms have ocean views. Rates include parking, a small breakfast, and tea.

Sunset Tower Hotel
MAP M3 ▪ 8358 Sunset Blvd ▪ 323-654-7100 ▪ www.sunsettowerhotel.com ▪ $$$

Once the home of John Wayne and mobster Bugsy Siegel, the Sunset Tower is a striking Art Deco tower. The former apartments are now luxuriously appointed rooms and suites, with reproductions of 1920s period furniture.

Chic and Hip Hotels

Avalon Hotel Beverly Hills
MAP K6 ▪ 9400 W Olympic Blvd ▪ 310-277-5221 ▪ www.viceroyhotelgroup.com/avalon ▪ $$

This Beverly Hills hotel has intimately lit cabanas that fringe the curvaceous pool. Rooms feature George Nelson lamps and Eames-style chairs. And don't forget – Marilyn Monroe once lived here.

Beverly Hilton
MAP J6 ▪ 9876 Wilshire Blvd ▪ 310-274-7777 ▪ www.beverlyhilton.com ▪ $$

Famous for hosting the annual Golden Globes, this mid-century landmark is frequented by the big shots of Hollywood. It features a saltwater aquarium in the lobby, Bose music systems, and large screen plasma TVs in the rooms as well as an innovative health and fitness retreat.

Élan Hotel
MAP L5 ▪ 8435 Beverly Blvd ▪ 866-203-2212 ▪ www.elanhotel.com ▪ $$

The lobby and lounge at this stylish boutique hotel is decorated in the retro look currently in vogue. The rooms have calming natural tones and it's close to some of the city's finest attractions. You can also order room service and pick a movie from the extensive library.

The Grafton on Sunset
MAP L3 ▪ 8462 W Sunset Blvd ▪ 323-654-4600 ▪ www.graftononsunset.com ▪ $$

Standing next to the Mondrian, the Grafton has a more accessible and low-key ambience. The lobby is flanked by the fashionable Balboa Lounge, and leads to the pool.

Maison 140
MAP J6 ▪ 140 Lasky Dr ▪ 310-281-4000 ▪ www.maison140.com ▪ $$

An intimate B&B in the former villa of silent movie star Lillian Gish, Maison 140 cleverly fuses French and Asian design accents. Every room is different, but all feature patterned wallpaper and European antiques. The seductively lit Bar Noir is great for a nightcap. Excellent value for money, considering its proximity to Rodeo Drive.

Mama Shelter
MAP Q2 ▪ 6500 Selma Ave, Hollywood ▪ 323-785-6666 ▪ www.mamashelter.com ▪ $$

This stylish, offbeat hotel is within walking distance of everything in Hollywood. This is a French-based chain and the decor is colorful, whimsical, and fun: you may just find a Darth Vader lamp in your room. iMacs substitute for TVs and radios. Don't miss the rooftop bar with views of the Hollywood Sign.

The Standard Hollywood
MAP M3 ▪ 8300 Sunset Blvd ▪ 323-650-9090 ▪ www.standardhotels.com ▪ $$

This hangout on Sunset Strip has a wavy retro facade and a pool with an intriguing fringe of blue Astroturf. After relaxing by the water, party in the lobby, which morphs into a lounge at night, with DJ-spun music.

W Los Angeles
MAP C2 ▪ 930 Hilgard Ave ▪ 310-208-8765 ▪ www.wlosangeles.com ▪ $$

The chic W is full of surprises, such as the "waterfall" entrance steps and the table games in the lobby. Suites are fully wired for connectivity, and the Mojo eatery and lobby bar are weekend hot spots.

The Jeremy West Hollywood
MAP L3 ▪ 8490 Sunset Blvd ▪ 310-424-1600 ▪ www.jeremyhotel.com ▪ $$$

The first hotel to be built from the ground up on the Strip in more than 30 years, this cool, stylish hotel sports a full gym, on-site café, business services and luxury, minimalist rooms and a rooftop pool and bar overlooking all of Downtown. The extensive art collection features some statement pieces from renowned artists.

Mondrian Hotel

MAP M3 ■ 8440 Sunset Blvd ■ 323-650-8999 ■ www.mondrianhotel. com ■ $$$

The rooms seem like an afterthought at hotelier Ian Schrager's celebrity outpost. The Ivory on Sunset eatery, the pool deck, and the hip SkyBar provide stylish hob nobbing territory.

Sunset Marquis Hotel & Villas

MAP L3 ■ 1200 N Alta Loma Rd ■ 310-657-1333 ■ www.sunsetmarquis. com ■ $$$

This West Hollywood hideaway (see p55) is a favorite with rock'n'roll royalty such as U2. The on-site recording studio is a major draw, but so are the luxurious quarters and the Bar 1200.

Viceroy

MAP B4 ■ 1819 Ocean Ave ■ 310-260-7500 ■ www.viceroyhotels andresorts.com/ santamonica ■ $$$

The couple behind the stylish Maison 140 and Avalon have created a fantasy environment that transports guests back in time to Colonial England. The decor mixes kitsch and sophistication, with a grown-up color palette of gray, bright green, and soothing cream.

Beach Hotels

Cadillac Hotel

MAP A4 ■ 8 Dudley Ave ■ 310-399-8876 ■ No air conditioning ■ www.the cadillachotel.com ■ $

Charlie Chaplin liked to spend summers in this pink-and-turquoise Art Deco landmark on Venice Boardwalk. Clean but basic rooms, including some four-bed dorms.

Beach House at Hermosa Beach

MAP A3 ■ 1300 The Strand ■ 310-374-3001 ■ www.beach-house. com/hermosa-beach ■ $$

Within earshot of the waves, this elegant getaway is the perfect antidote to stress. Just relax in front of the crackling fire in your suites.

Hotel Erwin

MAP B5 ■ 1697 Pacific Ave ■ 310-452-1111 ■ www. hotelerwin.com ■ $$

This boutique beach hotel is located close to Venice Beach and Santa Monica Pier and gives you easy access to interesting cafés and stores. Its 119 guestrooms come with the full range of amenities. The hotel has a fitness suite and rates include breakfast.

Jamaica Bay Inn

MAP B6 ■ 4175 Admiralty Way ■ 310-823-5333 ■ www.jamaicabayinn. com ■ $$

For beachfront on a budget, opt for this pleasant Marina del Rey hotel right on Mother's Beach. The sand-colored rooms have private patios or balconies.

Sea Sprite Motel & Apartments

MAP D4 ■ 1016 The Strand ■ 310-376-6933 ■ No air conditioning ■ www.seaspritemotel. com ■ $$

Rooms in this Hermosa Beach hotel won't win any style awards, but with their location right on the beach, you probably won't spend much time inside. Larger dorms can sleep up to six.

JW Marriott Santa Monica Le Merigot

MAP B4 ■ 1740 Ocean Ave ■ 310-395-9700 ■ www.marriott.com ■ $$$

Centrally located, this Santa Monica hotel has the elegant personality of a Mediterranean mansion. Rooms are dressed in sunny, golden colors and feature patios, heavenly beds, and big desks. Bold chandeliers light up the Cézanne restaurant, where you can taste exquisite French cuisine. Excellent in-house spa.

Malibu Beach Inn

MAP A2 ■ 22878 Pacific Coast Hwy ■ 310-456-6444 ■ www.malibu beachinn.com ■ $$$

Enjoy spectacular views of the coastline from Malibu's only luxury beachfront hotel with a red-tiled Mission-style building. All rooms have gas fireplaces and balconies, some also feature a Jacuzzi. A free Continental breakfast buffet is served.

Ritz-Carlton Marina del Rey

MAP B6 ■ 4375 Admiralty Way ■ 310-823-1700 ■ www.ritzcarlton.com ■ $$$

Overlooking the world's largest custom-built pleasure boat harbor, the Ritz-Carlton offers European elegance and deluxe creature comforts. Indulge in global cuisine at the stylish restaurant.

For a key to hotel price categories see p144

Shore Hotel
MAP A3 ▪ 1515 Ocean Ave ▪ 310-458-1515 ▪ www.shorehotel.com ▪ $$$
This hotel is just steps away from Santa Monica Pier. Rooms have private patios or balconies, and luxury bath products. Its Blue Plate Taco restaurant is a great place for outdoor dining and people-watching.

Shutters on the Beach
MAP A4 ▪ 1 Pico Blvd ▪ 310-458-0030 ▪ www.shuttersonthebeach.com ▪ $$$
This delightful hotel right by the sands of Santa Monica takes the beach cottage to new heights. Relax on fluffy mattresses, feel the cool ocean breeze, or watch the warm California sunlight filtering in through the shutters.

Business Hotels

DoubleTree by Hilton Hotel Los Angeles Downtown
MAP W4 ▪ 120 S Los Angeles St ▪ 213-629-1200 ▪ doubletree3.hilton.com ▪ $$
This serene Little Tokyo hotel offers an exotic experience, especially if staying in the Japanese rooms, where you sleep on tatami mats. The spa and the beautiful third-floor Japanese gardens are great for relaxing.

Los Angeles Airport Marriott
MAP D3 ▪ 5855 W Century Blvd ▪ 310-641-5700 ▪ www.marriott.com ▪ $$
Close to LAX, this chain hotel is great for business travelers. With just over 1,000 rooms, it has a full range of conference facilities, with business and secretarial services. All rooms have wireless internet access, and high-speed connection is available at an extra cost.

Luxe Hotel Sunset Boulevard
MAP C2 ▪ 11461 Sunset Blvd ▪ 310-476-6571 ▪ www.luxesunset.com ▪ $$
A lovely property with lush landscaping, the Luxe is conveniently located right next to Freeway 405. The spacious rooms are decorated in soothing colors. Business features include in-room tablets, complimentary Wi-Fi, and secretarial services.

Orlando Hotel
MAP M5 ▪ 8384 W 3rd St ▪ 323-658-6600 ▪ www.theorlando.com ▪ $$
Suitable for smaller gatherings, the trump card of this European-style hotel is its location close to the shopping and nightlife in West Hollywood and Beverly Hills. Rates include a daily taxi voucher.

The Westin Bonaventure Hotel & Suites
MAP U4 ▪ 404 S Figueroa St ▪ 866-716-8132 ▪ www.thebonaventure.com ▪ $$
With about 20 eateries, a pool, a fitness club, shops, and a full business center, the landmark Bonaventure has more facilities than most small towns. It is well located, only 1 mile (1.6 km) from the LA Convention Center.

Regular rooms here are fairly small, but the office suites are well equipped.

Hilton Checkers Hotel
MAP U5 ▪ 535 S Grand Ave ▪ 213-624-0000 ▪ www3.hilton.com ▪ $$$
An island of old-world sophistication in the fast-paced Financial District, this 1929 hotel is great for conducting business in style. Prepare for your meetings in fine leather chairs at exquisite large marble desks.

JW Marriott Los Angeles LA Live
MAP S6 ▪ 900 W Olympic Blvd ▪ 213-765-8600 ▪ www.marriott.com ▪ $$$
A short walk to the LA Convention Center, Staples Center and LA Live, this hotel has everything you need to conduct business. The gorgeous lobby is conducive to work, as are the 38 meeting rooms and the well-equipped business center. After work, relax at the rooftop pool and unwind with a drink at the bar. The gym is modern and Marriott guests have access to the Ritz-Carlton spa.

Loews Hollywood Hotel
MAP P2 ▪ 1755 N Highland Ave ▪ 323-856-1200 ▪ www.loewshotels.com/hollywood-hotel ▪ $$$
This art-filled high-rise overlooks Hollywood and Highland. The suites here can accommodate small meetings. An equipped business center, PC rentals, and secretarial services are also on offer.

Omni Los Angeles Hotel at California Plaza

MAP V4 ■ 251 S Olive St ■ 213-617-3300 ■ www. omnihotels.com ■ $$$
Walk to Walt Disney Concert Hall, MOCA, and other Downtown landmarks from this modern hotel in the Financial District. Business rooms have huge desks, office equipment, and supplies.

SLS Hotel at Beverly Hills

MAP L5 ■ 465 S La Cienega Blvd ■ 310-247-0400 ■ www.slshotels. com/beverlyhills ■ $$$
Friendly and efficient staff, a business center with high-speed internet access, and meeting rooms with assets such as teleconferencing and video equipment are just some of the great perks of this Beverly Hills hotel.

Family Hotels and Motels

Best Western Plus Hollywood Hills

MAP Q2 ■ 6141 Franklin Ave ■ 323-464-5181 ■ www.bestwestern.com ■ $
Other hotels may have more stylish rooms, but the ones at this central Hollywood property offer plenty of elbow space. The tiled pool and coffee shop are welcome assets.

Portofino Inn & Suites

MAP F4 ■ 1831 S Harbor Blvd ■ 714-782-7600 ■ www.portofinoinn anaheim.com ■ $
This spacious Anaheim hotel is great for wallet-watchers. The little ones will love camping out in bunk beds and a sofa sleeper and will get their own amenities such as TV, microwave, and fridge as well.

Cal Mar Hotel Suites

MAP A3 ■ 220 California Ave ■ 310-395-5555 ■ No air conditioning ■ www.calmarhotel.com ■ $$
The flowery bedspreads and sofas may be stuck in the 1980s, but you get an entire apartment for less money than a standard double anywhere else. Units face a landscaped pool. Located in a quiet residential street, Cal Mar is close to Santa Monica hip zones. Free parking is available.

The Garland

MAP D1 ■ 4222 Vineland Ave, North Hollywood ■ 818-238-3759 ■ www. beverlygarland.com ■ $$
This hotel is conveniently located close to Universal Studios. Special children's suites with bunk beds and play stations are available and breakfast is free for under 12s. Facilities include an outdoor pool, a gym and tennis courts.

Hotel Beverly Terrace

MAP K4 ■ 469 North Doheny Dr, Beverly Hills ■ 310-274-8141 ■ www. hotelbeverlyterrace.com ■ $$
Within walking distance of Rodeo Drive and Sunset Strip, this serene hotel has a garden and pool area and provides a welcome escape from the hustle and bustle of the city. Ideally located for shopping and dining.

Kimpton Hotel Palomar

MAP C2 ■ 10740 Wilshire Blvd ■ 310-475-8711 ■ www.hotelpalomar-lawestwood.com ■ $$
Located in Westwood village, this family hotel allows you easy access to shops, restaurants, and theaters. It includes a full-service restaurant, bar, swimming pool, gym, and gift shop.

Magic Castle Hotel

MAP P2 ■ 7025 Franklin Ave ■ 800-741-4915 ■ www.magiccastlehotel. com ■ $$
Pennywise travelers love this hotel close to Hollywood action. Units vary in size but have full kitchens. Guests also enjoy access to the nearby Magic Club.

Sheraton Universal Hotel

MAP D1 ■ 333 Universal Hollywood Dr ■ 818-980-1212 ■ www.starwood hotels.com ■ $$
Although this property can't shake off the institutional feel of a chain hotel, its location next to Universal Studios is a bonus.

Disney's Grand Californian Hotel

MAP F4 ■ 1600 S Disneyland Dr ■ 714-956-6425 ■ www.disneyland. com ■ $$$
The price tag is a bit steep at this 751-room resort designed in richly wooded Craftsman style, but standard rooms sleep up to two adults and four kids, and it even has its own private entrance to Disney's California Adventure™ (see pp38–9) theme park.

For a key to hotel price categories see p144

Loews Santa Monica Beach Hotel

MAP A3 ▪ 1700 Ocean Ave ▪ 310-458-6700 ▪ www.santamonica loewshotel.com ▪ $$$

Located very close to Santa Monica Pier and the beach, this large resort appeals to children, and is the definition of the quintessential Californian retreat, offering special welcome kits, and free stays for under 18s. The restaurant here serves the best seafood that Santa Monica has to offer.

Budget Hotels and Hostels

Beverly Laurel Motor Hotel

MAP M4 ▪ 8018 Beverly Blvd ▪ 323-651-2441 ▪ $

This 1950s-style motel with a small, seasonal pool is within walking distance of the Farmers Market, Melrose Avenue, and the Beverly Center. Framed art and cheerful bedspreads adorn the rooms. The downstairs diner, Swingers (see p113), is a popular spot. Parking and Wi-Fi are chargeable.

Highland Gardens Hotel

MAP P2 ▪ 7047 Franklin Ave ▪ 323-850-0536 ▪ www.highlandgardens hotel.com ▪ $

A large pool and tropical garden give this hotel near the Walk of Fame an old-Hollywood atmosphere. Rooms are basic, with fridges and complimentary Wi-Fi. Rates also include hot drinks in the lobby, parking, and Continental breakfast.

Hollywood Celebrity Hotel

MAP P2 ▪ 1775 Orchid Ave ▪ 323-850-6464 ▪ www.hotelcelebrity. com ▪ $

Despite the name, celebrity encounters are exceedingly unlikely in this budget gem, a stone's throw away from Hollywood & Highland. But the inviting burgundy awning and Art Deco lobby lead to nicely sized rooms with walls with cartoon-like murals. Rates include a small breakfast as well as on-site parking.

Hollywood Orchid Suites Hotel

MAP P2 ▪ 753 Orchid Ave ▪ 323-874-9678 ▪ www. orchidsuites.com ▪ $

This is an excellent base of for those wanting to be close to the action. Some of the suites offer all the amenities you would expect from a small apartment, complete with a full kitchen, living room, bedroom, and balconies. The decor may be dated, but it's all well kept and clean. The pool and rooftop sundeck are definite perks and this place offers good value.

Safari Inn

MAP D1 ▪ 1911 W Olive Ave ▪ 818-845-8586 ▪ www.coasthotels.com ▪ $

Easily recognized by its classic neon sign, this retro motel is nothing short of iconic. Rooms are decked out in peach and blue and some offer a full kitchen for convenience. Close to Universal, NBC, and Warner Bros Studios, with specific packages offered that include studio tours and other privileges.

Sea Shore Motel

MAP B4 ▪ 2637 Main St ▪ 310-392-2787 ▪ www. seashoremotel.com ▪ $

A Santa Monica budget abode, it is perfect for those who favor location over luxury. Only two blocks from the beach, it is on trendy Main Street with wonderful shopping and dining options.

Stillwell Hotel

MAP T5 ▪ 838 S Grand Ave ▪ 213-627-1151 ▪ www. stillwell-hotel.com ▪ $

One of the best bargains in Downtown LA, the Stillwell puts you within walking distance of the Staples Center. It's in a well-restored early 20th-century building and has a popular Indian restaurant and a graceful old-time cocktail lounge.

USA Hostels Hollywood

MAP Q2 ▪ 1624 Schrader Blvd ▪ 323-462-3777 ▪ www.usahostels.com ▪ $

Those traveling on a tight budget will find this friendly Hollywood hostel a good jumping-off place for their explorations. Rates include hot drinks, pancakes for breakfast, linen, and lockers.

Farmer's Daughter Hotel

MAP M5 ▪ 115 S Fairfax Ave ▪ 800-334-1658 ▪ www.farmersdaughter hotel.com ▪ $$

The "price is right" at this motel opposite the Original Farmers Market and CBS, which explains its popularity with game-show contestants taping at the TV studio. The staff will organize tickets if you'd like to be part of the audience.

Inn at Venice Beach
MAP B6 ■ 327 Washington Blvd ■ 310-821-2557 ■ www.innat venicebeach.com ■ $$
The beach beckons outside this small hotel on the border of Venice and Marina del Rey. Rooms offer moderate comforts and a cheerful decor. Breakfast included.

B&Bs

Elaine's Hollywood Bed & Breakfast
MAP N2 ■ 1616 N Sierra Bonita ■ 323-850-0766 ■ No credit cards ■ www. elaineshollywoodbedand breakfast.com ■ $
This beautifully restored 1910 bungalow has two rooms available and is located in a quiet neighborhood. Elaine's is a perfect base for exploring Hollywood and its gracious hosts will help you plan your outings.

Malibu Bella Vista
MAP A2 ■ 25786 Piuma Rd ■ 818-591-9255 ■ www.malibubella vista.com ■ $
Nestled in Malibu Canyon, the ranch-style Bella Vista is ideally located just minutes from the beach and good hiking trails. Spa facilities are available and the excellent Saddle Peak Lodge gourmet restaurant is close.

Secret Garden B&B
MAP M2 ■ 8039 Selma Ave ■ 323-656-3888 ■ Limited air-conditioning ■ www. secretgardenhollywood. com ■ $
Just a few steps from Sunset Strip, this Spanish-Mediterranean home has five unique rooms. The hosts whip up amazing breakfasts. One room is accessible for guests with specific needs.

Bissell House
MAP E1 ■ 201 Orange Grove Ave ■ 626-441-3535 ■ www.bissell house.com ■ $$
This stately 1887 Victorian home has a prestigious address on Pasadena's famed "Millionaire's Row." A sedate, grown-up atmosphere reigns in the elegant public areas and all eight cozy rooms. There is no disabled access here.

Channel Road Inn
MAP C2 ■ 219 W Channel Rd ■ 310-459-1920 ■ www.channelroad inn.com ■ $$
A Neo-Colonial home built in 1915, it is clad in wooden shingles and sits on the northern edge of Santa Monica. Each room has different perks such as fireplaces, lovely four-poster beds, patios, soaking tubs, or a view.

Dockside Boat & Bed
MAP E4 ■ 316 E Shoreline Dr ■ 562-436-3111 ■ Limited air-conditioning ■ www.boatandbed.com ■ $$
A unique getaway, this floating B&B has on offer a fully equipped sailboat, motor yacht, and even a Chinese junk. Boats are moored in Long Beach's Rainbow Harbor; enjoy views of the Queen Mary.

Hollywood Bed & Breakfast
MAP N2 ■ 1701 N Orange Grove Ave ■ 323-874-8017 ■ www.hollywood bandb.com ■ $$
Located in a residential area, this quiet six-room property has a private movie-screening room, parlor, dining room, outdoor pool, kitchen, and dance/exercise room to go with the traditionally decorated rooms. Also on offer here are free parking and Wi-Fi.

Venice Beach House
MAP A6 ■ 15 30th Ave ■ 310-823-1966 ■ www. venicebeachhouse.com ■ $$
Built in 1911 by relatives of Venice founder Abbot Kinney (see p122), this delightful inn is a witness to Venice history. A quiet oasis, it allows you to retreat to the comforts of cozy, antique-filled rooms after a busy day at the beach or in town.

Inn at Playa del Rey
MAP B7 ■ 435 Culver Blvd ■ 310-574-1920 ■ www. innatplayadelrey.com ■ $$$
Modern and breezy, this B&B is close to the ocean and Marina del Rey, and overlooks the Ballona Wetlands Ecological Reserve. Some rooms have Jacuzzis and fireplaces. Close to LAX airport, the B&B also offers free parking and bicycle rental.

Inn on Mt. Ada
MAP D7 ■ 398 Wrigley Rd ■ 310-510-2030 ■ No air-conditioning ■ www. innonmtada.com ■ $$$
Live it up in the grandeur of William Wrigley's former hilltop mansion on Catalina Island. Standard rates include breakfast, a light lunch, evening champagne reception, and the use of a golf car, so that you can explore around town.

For a key to hotel price categories see p144

General Index

Page numbers in **bold** refer to main entries.

A

Abalone Cove 123
Abbot Kinney Boulevard 7, 69
Abduction of Europa, The (Rembrandt) 17
Academy Museum of Motion Pictures 23
Accessories shops 111, 118
Accommodations 143, 144–51
ACME Comedy Theater 65
Adoration of the Magi, The (Mantegna) 16
Affleck, Ben 15, 55
Air travel 136, 137
Allen, Terry 82
Alys, Francis 21
América Tropical (Siqueiros) 24
American Cinematheque 60
Amusement parks *see* Theme and amusement parks
Andaz West Hollywood 14
Aniston, Jennifer 68
Apple Store 96
Aquarium of the Pacific 58
Arbuckle, Fatty 61
Architecture
    Art Deco on the Miracle Mile 23
    Downtown 81
    Getty Center 19
    landmarks 48–9
    Venice Boardwalk 124
ArcLight Cinemas 62
Around Downtown 84–9
    Exploring Exposition Park in a Day 87
    map 84
    places to eat 98
    sights 84–8
Art galleries (commercial)
    Chung King Road galleries 79
    Laguna Beach 132
    West Hollywood and Midtown 108, 110
    see also Museums and galleries
Artist's Garden at Vétheuil (Monet) 19
Astronaut Ellison S' Onizuka Memorial 82
ATMs 140
Audiences Unlimited 61
Autry Museum of the American West 34
Avalon 42
Avalon Casino (Catalina Island) 42

Aviation industry 46–7
Avila, Francisco 25
Avila Adobe 25

B

B&Bs 143, 151
Balboa Island 130, 131
Ball, Lucille 117
Baltimore, David 92
Banking 140
Banning, Phineas 47
Bar 1200 55
Bar Marmont 54, 109, 112
Barneys New York 55
Barnsdall, Aline 101
Bars and clubs
    Hollywood 102
    places to see and be seen 54–5
    Sunset Strip 112
Baseball 87
Basketball 55, 124
Beaches 50–51
    hotels 147–8
    safety 138
Beckett, Welton 101
Bel-Air *see* Beverly Hills, Westwood, and Bel-Air
Bellows, George 20
Belushi, John 15, 61
Benny, Jack 117
Bergamot Station 122
Beverly Hills Civic Center 115
Beverly Hills Hotel 114, 146
Beverly Hills, Westwood, and Bel-Air 114–19
    Tour of Stars' Homes, A 117
    map 114–15
    places to eat 119
    Rodeo Drive shops 118
    sights 114–17
Bicycling 126, 131, 137
Biddy Mason: A Passage Through Time (Saar/de Bretteville) 82
Big Red Cars (The Huntington) 31
Big Thunder Mountain Railroad (Disneyland) 36
Billboards, giant (Sunset Strip) 14
Bing Theater at LACMA 63
Blessing of the Animals (Politi) 24
Blue Boy (Gainsborough) 30
Bogart, Humphrey 15, 102
Bolsa Chica Ecological Reserve 129
Bono 55
Boogie boarding 126
Book Soup 55
Bookstores 55, 56, 60, 96, 125

Borofsky, Jonathan, *Molecule Man* 82
Boulle, André-Charles 16
Bow, Clara 117
Bradbury Building 7, 49, 79
Bradley, Tom 47
Brando, Marlon 63
Breakfast in Bed (Cassatt) 31
Brennan, Walter 63
Brewery Arts Complex 88
Broad Museum 6, 7, 80
Broadway Historic Theater District 81
Bronson Caves (Griffith Park) 35
Bruggen, Coosje van 49
Budget hotels 150–51
Budget tips 71
Buffalo 43
Bullocks Wilshire Building 88
Bunker Hill Steps 79, 81
Burden, Chris 23
Bus travel 136, 137
Business hotels 148–9

C

Cabrillo Beach 51
Cabrillo Marine Aquarium 58
Cafés *see* Bars and clubs; Restaurants
Calder, Alexander 53, 82
California Adventure® (Disneyland® Resort) 7, **38–9**
California African American Museum 86, 87
California Institute of Technology (CalTech) 92–3
California Science Center 58, 70, 86, 87
    Imax Theater 62, 87
Calydonian Boar Hunt, The (Rubens) 17
Canterbury Tales, The (Chaucer) 29
Capitol Records Tower 13
Car rental 71, 136
Car travel 136
Carlos III of Spain 24, 46
Cartier-Bresson, Henri 110
Casino Point Dive Park (Catalina Island) 43
Cassatt, Mary 20, 31
Catalina Country Club 43
Catalina Island 11, **42–3**, 123
Cathedrals
    Cathedral of our Lady of Angels 6, 49, 78, 79
    St. Sophia Cathedral 86
Cayton Children's Museum by ShareWell 59

Cell phones 140
Cemeteries 35, 71, 100, 117
Central Library 80
Cézanne, Paul 91
  *Young Italian Woman at a
  Table* 17
Chandler, Harry 24, 99
Channel Islands National
  Park 73
Chaplin, Charlie 15, 47, 62, 101
Charles F. Lummis Home &
  Garden 86–7
Charles Sumner Greene
  House 95
Chateau Marmont 15, 54, 145
Chaucer, Geoffrey 29
Chemosphere 49
Chiat/Day Building 49
Chic and hip hotels 146–7
Children
  attractions for 50–9
  Disneyland 40
Chimborazo (Church) 31
Chinatown 78, 79
Chinese American Museum 25
Christ's Entry into Brussels
  (Ensor) 17
Chung King Road galleries 79
Church, Frederic 31
Churches
  Angelus Temple 88
  Plaza Catholic Church 24–5
  Serra Chapel 130–31
  Wayfarer's Chapel 123
Cimarusti, Michael 66
Cinemark 18 & XD 62
Cinerama Dome 62, 101
Citrin, Josiah 67
City Hall 77
City Hall (Pasadena) 93
CityWalk (Universal Studios) 32
Clark, William Andrews Jr.
  88, 100
Clooney, George 54
Clooney, Rosemary 117
Clothing
  actors' 60
  Disneyland 40
  Fashion District 80
  places to see and be seen
  54–5
  stores 68–9, 96, 111, 118, 125
Coastal Orange County 128–33
  A Day in Balboa 131
  art experiences in Laguna
  Beach 132
  map 128
  places to eat 133
  sights 129–31
Coca-Cola Bottling Plant 81
Cole House 95
Colorado Street Bridge 93
Comedy & Magic Club, The 65
Comedy clubs 65
Comedy Store 65, 109
Comedy Union 65

Concerts, free 71
Constable, John 30
Consulates 138, 139
Copley, John Singleton 31
Coppola, Francis Ford 116
Corporate Head (Allen/Levine)
  82
Cosmetics 96
Craft & Folk Art Museum
  (CAFAM) 108
Craftsman houses 29, 57, 93,
  95
Crane, Cheryl 117
Crawford, Cindy 55
Credit & debit cards 140
Crime 139
Crosby, Bing 107
Crossroads of the World 101
Crowds (Disneyland) 40
Crystal Cove State Park 129
Currency 140
Customs regulations 138

D
Da Vinci, Leonardo 10
Dana, Richard Henry 130
Dana Point 130
Dance clubs (Hollywood) 102
Davis, Bette 35
Day trips 72–3
Day-Lewis, Daniel 63
De Bretteville, Sheila 82
De Mille, Cecil B. 12, 99, 100,
  107
De Palma, Brian 49
Dean, James 15, 34
Degas, Edgar 91
  Little Dancer Aged Fourteen
  94
Department stores 23, 55, 141
Depp, Johnny 15, 54, 107
Derrah, Robert 101
Diaz, Cameron 33
DiCaprio, Leonardo 55
DiMaggio, Joe 15
Disabled travelers 139
Discounts 71
Disney, Walt 41, 63
Disneyland® Resort 7, 11,
  36–41, 59
  California Adventure® 7, **38–9**
  hotels 40, 149
  practical tips 40, 71
  Walt Disney's vision 41
Diving & snorkeling (Catalina
  Island) 42, 43
Dodger Stadium 87
Doheny, Edward 47, 52
Dolby Theatre 13, 63, 65
Dolphins 129, 130
Domingo, Plácido 64
Doo Dah Parade 92
Douglas, Donald 46
Downtown 76–83
  architecture 81
  A Day in Downtown 79

Downtown (cont.)
  map 76–7
  places to eat 83
  public art 82
  sights 77–82
Downtown Art Walk 70
Downtown Arts District 80
DreamWorks Theater
  Featuring Kung-Fu
  Panda 33
Drives 72–3
Drug stores 139
Dubuffet, Jean 82
Duncan-Irwin House 95
Dürer, Albrecht 18

E
Eagle-Headed Deity 22
Earthquakes 47
Eastern Columbia Building
  81
Echigo 66, 113
Egyptian Theatre 13, 60, 62,
  101
El Capitan Theatre 13, 63, 101
El Matador Beach 50
El Pueblo de Los Angeles 6,
  7, 10, **24–5**, 77, 79
Electric Tram (Getty Center)
  18
Electrical appliances 141
Ensor, James 17
Entwistle, Peggy 99
Exotic Landscape (Rousseau)
  94
Exposition Park 87
  Rose Garden 52

F
Factor, Max 13
Fairbanks, Douglas Jr. 100
Fairbanks, Douglas Sr. 12, 47,
  100, 114
Falk, Peter 117
Family hotels 149–50
Farmers Market 7, 69, 107, 109
Fashion District 80
FASTPASS (Disneyland) 40
Festival of Arts and Pageant
  of the Masters (Laguna
  Beach) 132
Fine, Jud 82
Fine Arts Building 81
Fireworks (Disneyland) 37
Fishburne, Lawrence 101
Fishing 126
Fleiss, Heidi 61
Flower Day (Rivera) 22
Flower Market 80
Flynn, Errol 53, 61
Food shops 125
Football 90, 91
Ford Amphitheatre 64
Forest Lawn Memorial Park –
  Hollywood Hills 35
Four Arches (Calder) 82

Franklin D. Murphy Sculpture Garden 53, 116
Fred Segal 54, 111
Free attractions 70–71
Freeth, George 47

G

Gable, Clark 12
Gainsborough, Thomas 30
Gamble, David & Mary 49
Gamble House 49, 93, 95
Gandhi, Mahatma 53
Garbo, Greta 117
Gardner, Ava 117
Gas stations 71
Gay & lesbian community 108
Gehry, Frank 48, 49, 64, 78, 91, 124
Gershwin, George 65
Gershwin, Ira 117
Getty, J. Paul 16
Getty Center 10, **16–19**, 48, 70, 116–17
  architecture 19
  Family Room 59
  itineraries 6, 7
Getty Villa 17
Giacometti, Alberto 18
Gilmore family 107
Go Los Angeles Card 71
Goya, Francisco de 91
Grable, Betty 12
Graham, Robert 81, 82
Grammy Museum 80
Grand Canal, Venice, The (Turner) 30
Grand Central Market 7, 79
Grant, Hugh 61
Greek Theatre (Griffith Park) 34, 64
Green Pleasure Pier (Catalina Island) 42
Greene, Charles & Henry 29, 31, 49, 93, 95
Greystone Mansion & Gardens 52
Griffith, D.W. 47
Griffith, Griffith Jenkins 34
Griffith Observatory & Planetarium 35, 70, 74–5
Griffith Park 7, 11, **34–5**, 52
Griffith Park & Southern Railroad 35
Grizzly River Run (California Adventure®) 38
Groundlings, The 65
Grove, The 69, 107, 109
Guardians of the Galaxy – Mission BREAKOUT! (California Adventure®) 39
Gutenberg Bible 29

H

HaHa Café 65
Hale, George E. 93
Hale House 84

Halsted House 95
Hammer, Armand 116
Hang-gliding 126
Hardware stores 96
Haring, Keith 110
Harrison, Rex 117
Haunted Mansion (Disneyland) 36
Hawks House 95
Health 138
Hefner, Hugh 100, 117
Hemingway, Ernest 98, 101, 103
Hendrix, Jimi 15
Hepburn, Audrey 118
Hepburn, Katherine 63
Heritage Square Museum 84
Hermosa Beach 51, 123, 147
Hiking 70, 126, 129
Hirai, Isao 82
Hiroshige 91
Historic Hollywood Boulevard 6, 7, 10, **12–13**, 99
Historic hotels 145–6
History 46–7
Hockney, David 12, 22–3
Hokusai 91
Hollyhock House 49, 101
Hollywood 98–103
  Day with the Stars, A 101
  bars & dance clubs 102
  connections 60–61
  Golden Age 46
  map 98
  places to eat 103
  sights 99–101
Hollywood & Highland 13, 63, 69, 99
Hollywood Boulevard *see* Historic Hollywood Boulevard
Hollywood Bowl 64, 71, 100
Hollywood Forever Cemetery 100
Hollywood Heritage Museum 99
Hollywood High School 101
Hollywood Museum 13
Hollywood Roosevelt, The 12, 63, 101, 145
Hollywood Sign 6, 70, 99, 100, 101
Homeware shops 96, 111, 125
Hopper, Edward, *The Long Leg* 30
Horsley, David & William 46
Hostels 143, 150
Hotels
  beach 147–8
  budget 150–51
  business 148–9
  chic and hip 146–7
  Disney 40, 149
  family 149–50

Hotels (cont.)
  historic charmers 145–6
  luxury 144–5
  rates & booking 143
Hower, Winslow 20
Hughes, Howard 15, 114
Huntington, Henry E. 28, 29, 52, 91
Huntington, The 6, 7, 11, 31, 52, 91
Huntington Beach 129

I

Ice House, The 65
Immigration 138
Improv, The 65
In the Woods at Giverny (Monet) 20
Indiana Jones Adventure™ (Disneyland) 37
Inline skating 126
Institute of Contemporary Art LA (ICALA) 85
Insurance 138
Internet 140
Irises (Van Gogh) 16
Irwin, Robert 18
Isozaki, Arata 78
Itineraries
  Day at the Beach, A 123
  Day in Balboa, A 131
  Day in Hollywood, A 109
  Day with the Stars, A 101
  Tour of Stars' Homes, A 117
  Day in Downtown, A 79
  Exploring Exposition Park in a Day 87
  Exploring Historic Pasadena 93
  Four Days in Los Angeles 7
  Two Days in Los Angeles 6
  see also Tours
It's Tough to Be a Bug! (California Adventure®) 38
It's a Wrap! 60
Ivy, The 54, 113

J

Jackson, Peter 32
Jagger, Mick 15
James Culbertson House 95
Japanese American National Museum 78, 80
Jewelry District 80
Jewelry shops 111, 118, 125
Jody Maroni's Sausage Kingdom 7, 123, 124
Joplin, Janis 15
Jurassic World – The Ride (Universal Studios) 33

K

Kandinsky, Wassily 22
Kayaking 126
Kearny, Stephen Watts 47
Keaton, Buster 35

Keaton, Diane 117
Kennedy, John F. 49, 114
Kennedy, Robert F. 47, 114
Kidman, Nicole 54
King, B.B. 64
King, Rodney 47
King Kong (Universal Studios) 32
Kinney, Abbot 122, 124
Knott's Berry Farm 72
Koreatown 87

L

LA Aqueduct 46
La Brea Tar Pits 71, 109
LA Lakers 55
L.A. Live Sports and Entertainment District 79
LA Riots 47
La Tour, Georges de, *The Magdalene with the Smoking Flame* 22
Laemmle, Carl 32
Laguna Beach 130
  art experiences 132
Lam, Wilfredo 21
Lancaster, Burt 117
Larry Edmunds Bookshop 60
Lasky, Jesse 99
Lassie 12
Last Bookstore, The 56
Laugh Factory, The 65, 109
Lautner, John 49
Lawrence, Jennifer 54
Lawrence, Thomas, *Pinkie* 30
Leetag, Edgar 56
Levine, Philip 82
Lichtenstein, Roy 78, 110
Light rail 137
Lipchitz, Jacques, *Peace on Earth* 82
Little Dancer Aged Fourteen (Degas) 94
Little Tokyo 78
Long Leg, The (Hopper) 30
Lopez, Jennifer 55
Los Angeles Convention Center 79
Los Angeles County Museum of Art (LACMA) 7, 10, **20–23**, 107, 109
  Bing Theater 63
  free concerts 71
Los Angeles International Airport 48, 136, 137
Los Angeles Maritime Museum 57
Los Angeles Memorial Coliseum 87
Los Angeles Zoo 34, 59
Los Feliz 100
Lost property 139
Lover's Cove (Catalina Island) 42
Lummis, Charles 85, 86–7
Luxury hotels 144–5

M

McCormack, John 53
MacDonald, Richard 132
Madame Tussaud's Hollywood 101
Madonna and Child (van der Weyden) 30
Madonna and Child with Book (Raphael) 94
Magdalene with the Smoking Flame, The (La Tour) 22
Magritte, René 21
Main Library (Pasadena) 93
Main Street (Santa Monica) 7, 69
  boutiques 125
MAK Center for Arts and Architecture 48
Malaga Cove 123
Malibu Adamson House 121, 123
Malibu Lagoon State Beach 50
Malls 69, 107, 118
Manhattan Beach 51, 123
Mansfield, Jane 100
Mantegna, Andrea 16
Mapplethorpe, Robert 110
Margaret Herrick Library 61
Mariachi Plaza 88
Marina del Rey 122, 123
Marine Avenue (Balboa Island) 130, 131
Markets
  Farmers Market 7, 69, 107, 109
  Flower Market 80
  Grand Central Market 7, 79
  El Mercado 88
  Mercado La Paloma 87
Marston's 6, 93, 97
Martin, Steve 117
Marx, Groucho 100
Marx Brothers 12
Mason, Biddy 82
Matisse, Henri 21
Matsuhisa 67, 119
Matterhorn Bobsleds (Disneyland) 36
Maude 67
May Company Building 23
Meier, Richard 16, 19, 48, 116
Mélisse 67
Melrose Avenue 7, 68, 108, 109
  shops 111
Merry-Go-Round (Griffith Park) 35
Metro 137
  art 56
Michael, George 61
Michael's 67
Mickey Mouse
  hidden Mickeys 40
  meeting 36

Mickey's Fun Wheel (California Adventure®) 38–9
Microsoft Theater 65
Midtown *see* West Hollywood and Midtown
Millennium Biltmore Hotel 79, 81, 145
Miracle Mile 23
Miró, Joan 18, 82
Mission San Buenaventura 73
Mission San Fernando Rey de España 72
Mission San Gabriel Arcangel 72
Mission San Juan Capistrano 130–31
MOCA Geffen Contemporary 80
Modern Rome, Campo Vecchio (Turner) 17
Molecule Man (Borofsky) 82
Moneo, Rafael 49
Monet, Claude 17, 91, 94, 116
  In the Woods at Giverny 20
Monroe, Marilyn 12, 15, 102, 117
Montana Avenue 68
Moore, Henry 18
Motels 143, 149–50
Movies
  Day with the Stars, A 101
  Tour of Stars' Homes, A 117
  history 46, 47
  Hollywood connections 60–61
  movie theaters 62–3
  Walt Disney 41
Mulholland Drive 72
Mulholland Drive (Hockney) 22–3
Mulholland, William 46, 47, 72
Murals 24, 124
Murphy, Eddie 33, 55
Muscle Beach Venice 51, 124
Museums and galleries
  Academy Museum of Motion Pictures 23
  Autry Museum of the American West 34
  Boone Gallery (The Huntington) 29
  Broad, The 6, 7, 80
  California African American Museum 86, 87
  California Science Center 58, 70, 86, 87
  Catalina Island Museum 43
  Chinese American Museum 25
  Craft & Folk Art Museum (CAFAM) 108
  free entry 71
  Getty Center 6–7, 10, 48, 70, 116–17
  Getty Villa 17

Museums and galleries
(cont.)
Grammy Museum 80
Heritage Square Museum
84
Hollywood Heritage
Museum 99
Hollywood Museum 13
Huntington, The 6, 11,
28–31, 91
Japanese American
National Museum 78, 80
Laguna Art Museum 132
Laguna College of Art and
Design Gallery 132
Los Angeles County
Museum of Art (LACMA) 7,
10, 20–23, 107, 109
Los Angeles Maritime
Museum 57
Madame Tussaud's
Hollywood 101
MOCA Geffen
Contemporary 80
Museum of Contemporary
Art (MOCA) 6, 78, 79
Museum of Jurassic
Technology 57
Museum of Latin American
Art 56
Museum of Tolerance 117
Natural History Museum
58, 85, 87
Nixon Presidential Library
and Museum 73
Norton Simon Museum 91,
93, 94
Pacific Asia Museum 91
Page Museum at the La
Brea Tar Pits 109
Pasadena Playhouse 93
Petersen Automotive
Museum 108, 109
Ronald Reagan Presidential
Library and Museum 73
Santa Monica Art Museum
122
Southwest Museum of the
American Indian 85
Travel Town Museum 34
UCLA Hammer Museum 116
Velveteria 56
Wells Fargo History
Museum 80
Music Center 64, 79
Musso & Frank Grill 12, 101,
103
Myers, Mike 33

N

Natural History Museum 58,
85, 87
Nature Center at Avalon
Canyon (Catalina Island) 43
Nestor Film Company 46
Neutra, Richard 100

Neve, Felipe de 46, 47
New Beverly Cinema 62
Newport Beach 129, 130
Newspapers 140–41
Nicholas Canyon Beach 50
Nicholson, Grace 91
Nicholson, Jack 55, 63
Nixon, Richard 73
Nixon Presidential Library
and Museum 73
Nobu Matsuhisa 67
Northridge Earthquake
(1994) 47
Norton Simon Museum 91,
93, 94
Novo, The 79
Nuart Theatre, The 63

O

Off the beaten path 56–7
Oil industry 47
Old Bank District 81
Old Plaza 24
Old Plaza Firehouse 25
Old Town Pasadena 68, 93
Oldenburg, Claes 49
Olvera Street 24, 79
Opening hours 141
Orange County 128–33
Orozco, José Clemente 21
Oscars 13, 63, 65
Otis, Harrison Gray 47
Outdoor pursuits (Santa
Monica Bay) 126
Oviatt Building 81

P

Pacific Asia Museum 91
Pacific Design Center (PDC)
109
Pacific Theatres at The Grove
62
Page Museum at the La Brea
Tar Pits 109
Paley Center for Media 19, 116
Palisades Park 53, 123
Palos Verdes Peninsula 123
Pantages Theatre 12, 63, 64
Parades (Disneyland) 37
Paradise Cove 123
Paramount Ranch 57
Paramount Studios 99
tour 61, 99
Parking 71, 136, 137
Parks and gardens 52–53
Camellia Garden (The
Huntington) 28
Central Garden (Getty
Center) 18
Charles F. Lummis Home &
Garden 86–7
Chinese Garden (The
Huntington) 26–7, 28
Desert Garden (The
Huntington) 6, 28
Exposition Park 52, 87

Parks and gardens (cont.)
Franklin D. Murphy
Sculpture Garden 53, 116
Greystone Mansion &
Gardens 52
Griffith Park 7, 11, 34–5, 52
Huntington, The 6, 7, 11,
28–9, 52
Japanese Garden (The
Huntington) 28
North Vista (The
Huntington) 28
Palisades Park 53, 123
Rose Garden (Exposition
Park) 52
Rose Garden (The
Huntington) 6, 28
Runyon Canyon Park 53
Self-Realization Fellowship
Lake Shrine 53
South Coast Botanic
Garden 123
Virginia Robinson Gardens 52
Wrigley Mansion & Gardens
52, 92
Wrigley Memorial &
Botanic Gardens (Catalina
Island) 42
see also Theme and
amusement parks
Pasadena 90–97
Craftsman houses by
Greene & Greene 95
Exploring Historic
Pasadena 93
map 90–91
Norton Simon Museum
artworks 94
places to eat 97
shopping in Old Pasadena 96
sights 91–5
Pasadena Civic Center 92
Pasadena Playhouse 93
Passes 71, 137
Passports 138, 139
Patina 66
Payne, Edgar 132
Peace on Earth (Lipchitz) 82
Pelli, Cesar 109
Pereira and Luckman 48
Performing arts venues 64–5
Pershing Square 79
Personal security 139
Petersen Automotive
Museum 108, 109
Phoenix, River 15
Picasso, Pablo 21, 94
Pickford, Mary 47
Picnics 71
Pico, Pio 25
Pico House 25
Pierce Brothers Westwood
Village Memorial Park 117
Pinkie (Lawrence) 30
Pirates of the Caribbean
(Disneyland) 36

Pixar Pier (California Adventure®) 38
Places to see and be seen 54–5
Point Vicente 123
Politi, Leo 24
Pollock, Jackson 78
Portrait of Mrs Edward L. Davis and Her Son, Livingston Davis (Sargent) 22
Portrait of a Peasant (Van Gogh) 94
Postal services 140, 141
Presley, Elvis 12
Providence 66
Public art 82, 132
Public transportation 136–7
Puck, Wolfgang 54
Puppets 59

Q

Queen Mary 73
Quinn, Anthony 117

R

Radiator Springs Racers (California Adventure®) 39
Radio 140–41
Rail travel 136, 137
arrival of the railroad 46
Rainbow Bar & Grill 15, 112
Ranney House 95
Raphael 94
Ray, Man 18
Reagan, Ronald 73
Redondo Beach 50, 123
Rembrandt 17, 91, 94
Renoir, Auguste 17, 91
Restaurants 66–7, 142–3
Around Downtown 89
Beverly Hills, Westwood, and Bel-Air 119
Coastal Orange County 133
Downtown 83
Getty Center 18
Hollywood 103
Pasadena 97
places to see and be seen 54–5
Santa Monica Bay 127
West Hollywood and Midtown 113
Revenge of The Mummy – The Ride 3-D (Universal Studios) 33
Riots 47
Rivera, Diego 22
Roberts, Julia 15
Robertson Boulevard 68
Rodeo Drive 6, 68, 115
shops 118
Rodia, Simon 56
Rodin, Auguste 53, 91
Roger Rabbit's Car Toon Spin (Disneyland) 36
Rogers, Will 114

Ronald Reagan Presidential Library and Museum 73
Roosevelt, Franklin D. 57
Rose, Guy 110
Rose Bowl, The 90, 91
Ross, A.W. 23
Rousseau, Henri 94
Royce Hall 65
Rubens, Peter Paul 17
Runyon Canyon Park 53

S

Saar, Betye 82, 110
Safety
personal security 139
travel safety advice 138, 139
Sailing 122, 126
Samuel French Theatre & Film Bookshop 60
San Antonio Winery 85
San Clemente 128, 129
San Fernando Valley 72
Santa Barbara 73
Santa Monica 7, 120, 121–3
Santa Monica Art Museum 122
Santa Monica Bay 120–27
map 120–21
outdoor pursuits 123, 126
places to eat 127
sights 121–3
unique Main Street boutiques 125
Venice Boardwalk attractions 124
Santa Monica Beach 51
Santa Monica Mountains 72
Santa Monica Pier 51, 59, 121, 123
Santa Ynez 73
Santee Alley 69
Sargent, John Singer 22
Sawdust Art Festival (Laguna Beach) 132
Scandals 61
Schindler House 48
Schindler, Rudolph 48
Schoonhoven, Terry 82
Schwab's Pharmacy, Site of 15
Seal Beach 129
Self-Help Graphics & Arts 88
Self-Portrait (Rembrandt) 94
Self-Realization Fellowship Lake Shrine 53
Selvaggio, Piero 67
Senior discounts 71
Sepulveda, Eloisa 24
Sepulveda House 24
Serra, Junípero 47, 130
Shiva as the Lord of Dance 23
Shiva and Parvati 94
Shopping 142
Getty Center 18
Main Street (Santa Monica) 125
malls 69
Melrose Avenue 111

Shopping (cont.)
Old Pasadena 96
places to see and be seen 54–5
Rodeo Drive 118
streets 68–9
Shows (Disneyland) 37
Shrine Auditorium 63, 88
Siegel, Bugsy 15, 117
Sierra Madre 57
Silver Lake 100
Simpson, O.J. 61
Simpsons Ride™, The (Universal Studios) 32
Sinatra, Frank 117
Single lines (Disneyland) 40
Siqueiros, David Alfaro 24
Six Flags Magic Mountain 72
Skirball, Jack 115
Skirball Cultural Center 115
Smoking 139
Soarin' Around the World (California Adventure®) 39
Sony Pictures Studio Tour 61
Source Figure (Graham) 82
South Bay 123
South Coast Botanic Garden 123
Southern Pacific Railroad 31, 46
Souvenirs (Disneyland) 40
Space Mountain (Disneyland) 37
Spago Beverly Hills 54, 67, 119
Spine (Fine) 82
Splash Mountain (Disneyland) 37
Splichal, Joachim 66
Stammheim Missal 18
Standing Warrior 22
Stanwyck, Barbara 107
Staples Center 55, 79
Star Tours – The Adventure Continues (Disneyland) 37
Stark, Ray & Fran 18
Sterling, Christine 24
Stewart, Jimmy 117
Still Life with Lemons, Oranges, and a Rose (Zurbarán) 94
Stompanato, Johnny 117
Stone, Curtis 67
Street performers 124
Subway 137
Sunset Boulevard 14, 15
Sunset Plaza 14
Sunset Strip 6, 10, 107, 109
Sunset Strip Tattoo 15
Sunset Tower Hotel 15, 146
Surfing 125, 126, 129
Surfrider Beach 50, 123
Swedenborg, Emanuel 123

T

Tate, Sharon 61
Taxis 137

TCL Chinese Theatre 6, 8–9, 12, 63, 99, 101
Telephones 140
Television 140–41
  show audiences 70
Temple, Shirley 63
Theaters
  comedy 65
  movie 62–3
  performing arts venues 64–5
  tickets 71
Theatricum Botanicum 64
Theme and amusement parks
  Disneyland® Resort 7, 11, **36–41**
  Knott's Berry Farm 72
  Newport Fun Zone 131
  Pacific Park (Santa Monica) 59, 121
  Six Flags Magic Mountain 72
  Universal Studios Hollywood 7, 11, **32–3**
Theme Building at Los Angeles International Airport 48
Third Street Promenade 68, 121
Throop, Amos G. 92–3
Tickets
  budget tips 71
  public transportation 137
Tiepolo, Giovanni Battista 94
Time difference 141
TMZ Hollywood Tour 60
Torres-Garcia, Joaquin 21
Tourist information 142, 143
Tournament of the Roses 90, 91, 92
Tours
  drives and day trips 72–3
  movie 60–61
  trips and tours 142, 143
  see also Itineraries
Toy Story Midway Mania! (California Adventure®) 38
Travel
  getting there & around 136–7
  safety advice 138, 139
Travel Town Museum 34
Traveler (Schoonhoven) 82
The Triumph of Virtue and Nobility over Ignorance (Tiepolo) 94
Trolleys 31
Turner, J.M.W. 17, 30
Turner, Lana 61, 117
Twelve Months of the Year 107
Two Harbors (Catalina Island) 43

U

UCLA Hammer Museum 116
Union Station 77, 79

Universal Studios Hollywood 7, 11, **32–3**, 58
University of California, Los Angeles (UCLA) 104–5, 116
University of Southern California (USC) 87, 88
Untitled Improvisation III (Kandinsky) 22
Upright Citizens Brigade Theatre 65
Urban Light (Burden) 23
Urth Caffè 55
US Bank Tower 81
US–Mexican War 46

V

Valentino 67
Valentino, Rudolph 62, 100
Van Gogh, Vincent
  Irises 16
  Portrait of a Peasant 94
Van Rossem-Neill House 95
Vasquez Rocks 57
Velveteria 56
Venice Beach 44–5, 51
Venice Boardwalk 7, 122, 123
  attractions 124
Venice Canals 122
Venice Pier 124
Ventura 73
View on the Stour near Dedham (Constable) 30
Viper Room, The 15, 54, 107, 112
Virginia Robinson Gardens 52
Visas 138, 139

W

Walk of Fame 12, 13, 99
Walking 137
Walt Disney Concert Hall 6, 7, 48, 64, 78, 79
Warhol, Andy 78, 110
Warner Bros Tour 60
Washington, Denzel 55
Water, drinking 139
Water Grill 66, 83
Water World® (Universal Studios) 33
Watts Riots (1965) 47
Watts Tower 56
Wayne, John 117
Weather 141
Weinstein, Harvey 61
Wells Fargo Court 82
Wells Fargo History Museum 80
Wendt, William 132
West Hollywood and Midtown 106–13
  Day in Hollywood, A 109
  art galleries 110
  map 106
  places to eat 113

West Hollywood and Midtown (cont.)
  shops on Melrose Avenue 111
  sights 107–9
  Sunset Strip bars & clubs 112
West Third Street 69
Western Brothers, The (Copley) 31
Westin Bonaventure Hotel 81
Westwood see Beverly Hills, Westwood, and Bel-Air
Weyden, Rogier van der 30
Whales 129, 130
Wheatstacks, Snow Effect, Morning (Monet) 17
Whisky a Go-Go 15, 112
White Sisters House 95
Wildlife
  Bolsa Chica Ecological Reserve 129
  Cabrillo Marine Aquarium 58
  Catalina Island 42
  Long Beach Aquarium of the Pacific 58
  Los Angeles Zoo 34, 59
  Nature Center at Avalon Canyon (Catalina Island) 43
William Andrews Clark Memorial Library 88
Wilshire Boulevard 23
Wiltern, The 88
Windsurfing 126
Windward Avenue 124
Wine
  San Antonio Winery 85
  Wine Country 73
"Witch's House" 117
Wizarding World of Harry Potter, The (Universal Studios) 33
Woman with a Book (Picasso) 94
Women travelers 139
Wood, Natalie 117
World of Color (California Adventure®) 39
Wright, Frank Lloyd 79, 92, 100, 123
  Anderton Court 115, 118
  Hollyhock House 49, 101
Wrigley, William Jr. 42, 52
Wrigley Mansion & Gardens 52, 92
Wrigley Memorial & Botanic Gardens (Catalina Island) 42
Wyland, Robert 132
Wyman, George 49

Y

Yama and Yami 22
Young Italian Woman at a Table (Cézanne) 17

Z

Zappa, Frank 117
Zuma Beach 50, 123
Zurbarán, Francisco de 94

Acknowledgments

Author
Catherine Gerber has observed and documented the evolution of Los Angeles in both word and image for decades. She remains fascinated by her adopted home's ability to continuously and unapologetically reinvent itself. Her work has appeared in books, newspapers, and magazines in the USA and Europe.

Additional contributor
Pamela Barrus

Publishing Director Georgina Dee

Publisher Vivien Antwi

Design Director Phil Ormerod

Editorial Ankita Awasthi Tröger, Michelle Crane, Rachel Fox, Freddie Marriage, Sally Schafer, Rachel Thompson, Penny Walker

Cover Design Maxine Pedliham, Vinita Venugopal

Design Tessa Bindloss, Sunita Gahir, Bharti Karakoti, Rahul Kumar, Bhavika Mathur, Marisa Renzullo, Ankita Sharma, Priyanka Thakur, Vinita Venugopal

Picture Research Subhadeep Biswas, Ellen Root, Rituraj Singh

Cartography Zafar ul Islam Khan, Suresh Kumar, James Macdonald, Casper Morris

DTP Jason Little

Production Luca Bazzoli

Factchecker Carolyn Patten

Proofreader Clare Peel

Indexer Helen Peters

Revisions Nayan Keshan, Sumita Khatwani, Shikha Kulkarni, Meghna, Arushi Mathur, Bandana Paul, Azeem Siddiqui, Stuti Tiwari

Picture Credits

123RF.com: anilgrover 107b; Jon Bilous 53br; Michael Rosebrock 99cra.

4Corners: Susanne Kremer 3tl, 74–5.

Alamy Stock Photo: 504 collection 46bl; Rodolfo Arpia 42br; Calamy stock images 133bl; culliganphoto 3tr, 134–5; Ian G Dagnall 25tl, 49tl, 72clb, 81bl; Granger Historical Picture Archive 46cra; Brenda Kean 76tl; Robert Landau 10clb, 15br, 69cl; LHB Photo, 86t, 108c, 120tl; NiKreative 77br; Sean Pavone 1, 4t; Jamie Pham 26–7, 52cla, 4cr, 70cr, 80cl, 82tc, Photos 12 61tr; Prisma Bildagentur AG 4cl; Robertharding 92tr; robertharding / Richard Cummins 24–5c, RGB Ventures / SuperStock 63tr; RooM the Agency 4clb; Neil Setchfield 84cla; WENN Ltd 68cra; Nik Wheeler 72tr.

Andaz West Hollywood: 14cl.

Autry National Center: 34cla.

Baco Mercat: Dylan + Jeni 83cra.

Bar 1200: 55clb.

Barnsdall Art Park: 101cla.

Bijan: 118t.

Boardner's: 102t.

Border Grill Restaurant: 127cr.

California Science Center Foundation: 58cl.

University of Southern California: USC University Communications 88b.

Caro Bambino: 125cl.

Digital image courtesy of the Getty's Open Content Program: 16cr, 16bl, 17tl, 17cr, 18bc.

© Disney: 11bl, 36clb, 36–7, 37crb, 39crb, 40clb, 41tl; Paul Hiffmeyer 40tl, 40cr; © 1954 Disney 41b; Matt Stroshayne 39t.

Distant Lands—A Traveler's Bookstore & Outfitters: 96cla.

Dreamstime.com: Albertocc311 24br; Americanspirit 87bl; Riansho 100t; Jon Bilous 124b, 128c, Gerry Boughan 14–5c, 23bl, 55br, 70tl, 78b, 116tr; Nicholas Burningham 126cra; Dahlskoge 11cra; Ivan Dan 98tl; Foster Eubank 130cla; F11photo 19b; Enrique Gomez 69tr; Jorg Hackemann 70bl; Supannee Hickman 59t; Heather Jones 43crb; Kongomonkey 50clb; Erik Lattwein 65tr; Chon Kit Leong 92b; Lilyling1982 104–5, 123cla; Littleny 12clb 68b; Wei Chuan Liu 4b; David Lockeretz 42–3; Marcorubino 65tl; Meinzahn 13tl; Rick Moulton 73b; Juan Moyano 115t, 11cl, 99b; Natashabishop 11crb; Sarah Neveu 35crb; Kevin Panizza 43tl; Sean Pavone 12–3c, 11cl, 99b; Razyph 6cla; Alexander Reitter 122cl; Franco Ricci 2tr, 19cl, 44–5; Rui G. Santos 114cl; Starforeman 48b; Tupungato 10bc, 53tr,79cl; Wellesenterprises 54bl; Jeff Whyte 38b; Wiktor Wojtan 10bla, Ken Wolter 18tl, 57b, 61cl, 77tr, 92cl, 131tl; Wolterk 109cl; Zepherwind 129bl; Zverava 100t.

Courtesy of the Fahey/Klein Gallery, Los Angeles: 110b.

The Gamble House: Alexander Vertikoff 95b.

Getty Images: Gabriel Bouys 25cl; Richard Cummins 82clb, 86clb; Kevork Djansezian 71br; Stefanie Keenan 112br; Lonely Planet 71tl; Mathew Imaging 100clb; David Sucsy 34–5, 90r.

Gold Bug: 96br.

Hollywood Roosevelt Hotel: 12br.

The Huntington Library, Art Collections, and Botanical Gardens: 11tr, 28br, 28–9, 29tc, 30tl, 30crb, 31b.

iStockphoto.com: anouchka 62cla, csfotoimages 126bl; davidf 106cla; Marcus Lindstrom 53t; narvikk 62b; S. Greg Panosian 93clb; Ron Thomas 122b, 130–1; tobiasjo 121cr.

The Ivy: 54t, Richard Irving 113cr.

jAdis: 125crb.

Kelly Wearstler: 111c.

La Grande Orange Cafe: 97tr.

The Last Bookstore: James Martinez 56tr.

Los Angeles Philharmonic Association: 64br; Federico Zignani 64cla.

Los Angeles Zoo: Jamie Pham 59br.

Lucques: Rob Stark 113tl.

Maya Jewelry: 111cl.

Michael's: 67tr.

Millennium Biltmore hotel: 81tr.

MOCA The Museum of Contemporary Art, Los Angeles: Elon Schoenholz 78tl.

© Norton Simon Art Foundation: 94tr, 94bc.

Norton Simon Museum, Pasadena, Ca: 91tr.

Petersen Automotive Museum: 108t.

Photo © Museum Associates/ LACMA: 10bl, 20cl, 20crb, 21tl, 21crb, 22tr, 22clb, 23tc, 107tr.

Pig 'n' Whistle: 103clb.

Polo Lounge: 119clb.

Providence: Noe Montes 66c.

Rex by Shutterstock: 117clb; Everett Collection 47tr; Stock Connection 47clb.

Robert Harding Picture Library: Eye Ubiquitous 28cl; Gavin Hellier 4crb; H. & D. Zielske 4cra.

Samuel French Theatre & Film Bookshop: 60bl.

San Antonio Winery: 85t, 89cla.

Sawdust Art Festival: 132cla.

SkyBar: 112cla.

Southwest Museum of the American Indian: 85cb.

SuperStock: All Canada Photos / Robert Postma 129cra; Citizen of the Planet 34br, 49crb.

TCL Chinese Theatre IMAX: 2tl, 8–9, 63cl.

El Tepeyac Cafe é: 89cb.

UCLA Hammer Museum: 116cl.

Universal Studios Hollywood: 7br, 32br, 32–3, 33tl; Zack Lipp 33cr.

Valentino Restaurant: 67bl.

Velveteria: 56cl.

Viper Room: 15tl.

Warner Bros Studio Tour Hollywood: 60t.

Water Grill: 66t.

Cover
Front and spine: **Alamy Stock Photo:** Sean Pavone.

Back: **123RF.com:** Fabio Formaggio tl, tr; **Alamy Stock Photo:** Sean Pavone b; **iStockphoto.com:** LPETTET crb, Art Wager cla.

Pull Out Map Cover
Alamy Stock Photo: Sean Pavone.

All other images © Dorling Kindersley
For further information see: www.dkimages.com

As a guide to abbreviations in visitor information blocks: **Adm** = admission charge

Penguin
Random
House

Printed and bound in China

First edition 2004

Published in Great Britain by
Dorling Kindersley Limited
80 Strand, London WC2R 0RL

Published in the United States by
DK US, 1450 Broadway, Suite 801,
New York, NY 10018, USA

Copyright © 2004, 2019 Dorling
Kindersley Limited

A Penguin Random House Company

19 20 21 22 10 9 8 7 6 5 4 3 2 1

**Reprinted with revisions 2006, 2008, 2010,
2012, 2014, 2017, 2019**

A CIP catalog record is available
from the British Library.

A catalog record for this book is available
from the Library of Congress.

ISSN 1479-344X
ISBN 978-0-2413-6795-7